PRACTICAL

PROPAGATION

PRACTICAL
PROPAGATION

SALLY GREGSON

THE CROWOOD PRESS

First published in 2008 by
The Crowood Press Ltd
Ramsbury, Marlborough
Wiltshire SN8 2HR

www.crowood.com

British Library Cataloguing-in-Publication Data

A catalogue record for this book is available from the British Library.

ISBN 978 1 86126 989 8

Typeset by Florence Production Ltd, Stoodleigh, Devon

Printed and bound in Malaysia by Times Offset (M) Sdn Bhd

ACKNOWLEDGEMENTS

I have had a great deal of help and encouragement from family and friends in the course of writing this book. In particular, I would like to mention my husband, Peter, for all his patience and support. Also I would especially like to thank Tessa Forbes, lately of Plaxtol Nurseries, Kent, who laboriously read through the proofs. Additionally, my thanks to Henry Rothwell for his advice and work with the digital images, Bridget Beatty and Anne Wood for allowing me to photograph their lovely gardens, to Phillip Hodges, owner of Cheddar Garden Centre, Somerset, for allowing me to photograph potting sheds, frames, pots and sundries. I owe my basic knowledge of propagation to the tutors at Hadlow College, Kent, where I trained in Nursery Practice in the early 1980s.

Contents

Introduction

Plant propagation is a highly addictive pastime. That first tray of seedlings or row of rooted cuttings imparts such a deep satisfaction that it can only be matched by another tray or row of happy young plants. And, once hooked, the novice propagator is eager for more, as are friends, neighbours and family on the receiving end of such bounty. But, as in all things, the more that is learned, the greater is the awareness of how much more there is to know.

This book is not a list of plants and how to propagate each one. That would not be practical: there are currently over 70,000 different plants in commerce in the UK alone. Rather, it aims to help to determine which method of propagation to choose and to describe that method in detail. Prac-tice and experience will then bring the confidence to tackle any of those 70,000 plants.

One of the first dilemmas to face the novice propagator is whether to collect the seed of a particular plant, or to take cuttings, or to divide it up. As we will see, it all depends on the plant. Collecting seed seems the natural way of making more of the same plant and in the wild it mostly is. Dandelions and daisies have no trouble making more of themselves in the garden. Many plants seed themselves prolifically into gravel and cracks in the paving with great abandon.

We grow vegetables each year mostly from seed, as well as annual bedding plants and many herbs. There is a little diversity between individual plants,

Erigeron karvinskianus
self-sown into paved steps.

but on the whole they are very similar and good enough to cook or fill a hanging basket. The first part of this book deals with propagation by seed.

Seeds are remarkable things. Each seed contains a set of genes that will replicate most of its parents' features, but not all of them: hence the slight diversity in the row of cabbages or sweet peas. Just like children. We do not expect our offspring to be exact copies of either parent: each is different, be it hair colour, height or shape. Each child has its own random genetic mix. Each is unique.

Over the millennia, since people settled down and farmed the land, crop seed has been collected for sowing the following year. Naturally, only seed of the best crops has been selected to save: the fattest ears of grain; the largest beans; the tastiest carrots. Sometimes seed failed to germinate. Sometimes the crop succumbed quickly to disease. So in this way,

the seed with the most desirable genes has unwittingly been selected, resulting in bigger and better harvests each year; over time, seed has become easier to germinate and more disease-resistant. Consequently, we are the inheritors of vegetable seed that is nourishing, disease-resistant and, above all, easy to germinate.

Other plants we grow in our gardens have different family histories. Annual bedding plants have been deliberately bred and selected by seed merchants for no more than a hundred years or so, but are as easy as vegetable seed to germinate and grow or they would not be commercially viable. Annuals can only be propagated by seed and by definition have to be sown each year. However, few gardeners buy seed of the same perennial plants every year. There is no need, as perennial plants should last for years. The seed of shrubs and trees

Annual plants grown from seed.

can be tricky to germinate and most gardens would be too small to encompass a forest of birches or a plantation of Japanese acers. And few gardeners would even think of growing roses from seed: they are aware of the centuries of breeding that have produced that perfect hybrid tea.

Some of our garden plants that grow in the accommodating maritime climate of the UK hail from very different environments. Countries nearer the equator have more equal hours of day and night, less seasonal temperature change and altogether more heat. As a result, although some of the plants from these countries are obliging enough to grow and flower in the UK, often they fail to set seed.

But, most importantly, very many of the plants we grow in our gardens are selected hybrids. This means that a plant breeder has fertilized a particular flower with pollen from another particular flower and then grown on the resulting seedlings until they too produce flowers. The breeder then chooses one particular plant for colour, vigour, height, scent and health, then gives it a cultivar name: *Papaver orientale* 'Patty's Plum', for example. However, were the breeder then to sow the seed of *P.o.* 'Patty's Plum', the genes would be remixed and the result would not be *P.o.* 'Patty's Plum', but another row of different poppies.

So plants named with genus (*Papaver*), species (*orientale*) and cultivar name between inverted commas ('Patty's Plum') have to be propagated clonally, that is by division or root cuttings, and not from seed. The genetic mix has to be identical to reproduce the lovely crushed damson colour of the petals of this magnificent perennial poppy. And this is where the ingenuity and skill of the plant propagator comes in. Or a good hybrid may appear naturally in the nursery, be spotted by someone and then named: for example, *Verbascum* 'Helen Johnson' was found by Helen Johnson working in a commercial nursery in the UK.

The second part of this book sets out to categorize, as far as possible, the different sorts of plants and how and when to propagate each category clonally, from different sorts of cuttings and division.

But producing new plants does not end with sowing the seed or taking the cuttings; it involves potting them up and looking after them until they are big enough to leave home and tough it out

Seeds from an unusual coloured Papaver orientale . . .

. . . produce one that is an exceptional colour.

This Papaver orientale *is then propagated clonally and can be given a cultivar name.*

among their neighbours. The aftercare involved with each process of propagation is explained in detail. And despite all our efforts, however well-executed, there is always some bug or beastie that will come along and infect or eat our young plants. A separate section is devoted to the detection, prevention and, sometimes, the cure for each affliction.

Finally, the equipment and tools that are needed, as well as some that may not be entirely necessary but certainly desirable, are also covered in detail.

PART 1

Propagation by Seed

INTRODUCTION

Seeds are everyday wonders: small packages of genetic code, each an individual. These little parcels can vary in size from orchid seed that is as fine as dust, to big hairy coconuts. Each plant produces its own distinct seed design, from spiky grass seed, to winged sycamores, to rose seed contained within tasty red rosehips. Each design reflects its means of distribution to another site where the seed can germinate and colonize a new area, preventing competition and overcrowding.

The light weight of orchid seed means that it will float away on the merest hint of a breeze. Coconuts are transported by the sea to wash up on another tropical beach. And everyone is familiar with syca-more seed that produces its own helicopter blades to power it away to pastures new. Cyclamen seed is covered in a sweet, sticky gum that is attractive to ants. They pick them up and bear them off to bury in the path or the grass, where they can return to

feast on them if they could just remember where they put them.

Many of the grass seeds cling to animal fur, while sweet red berries attract animals, insects and birds to eat them and deposit the hard inner seed that has been softened by stomach acid elsewhere in a nutritious pile of dung. Some seed cases, such as hardy geraniums (cranesbills), explode violently, flinging their contents far and wide.

We can see, therefore, that most plants endeavour to send their offspring away so that each seed will germinate in its own space and not compete with its parent. Many plants, especially trees, actively put out a hormone that prevents their own seedlings from thriving within their root run. Horse chestnuts, for example, are rarely crowded out by their own offspring and neither are hellebores.

Seeds are also time machines. Those capsules of genetic code can lie dormant for centuries. In the late 1930s, seeds of a subtropical lotus were dug up in Northern China from the base of a lake that had

Packets of commercial seed.

Cyclamen coum seedlings flowering in a garden path.

dried up 250 years ago and sent to the University of Tokyo. Usually lotus seed is difficult to germinate, but 100 per cent germination occurred. A carbon-14 dating test on the seed indicated that it was 1,000 years old.

Understanding a little about the climate of the areas that seed originates from; about how the seed is distributed; and whether and how to store that seed, is clearly going to help with successful germination. Plant encyclopaedias that describe where a particular species originates from are very useful and a dictionary of plant names can be equally helpful (*see* Suggested Further Reading). Botanical Latin often seems at first bewildering and difficult to pronounce (but it's not a language and there is no correct way to say a botanical name). However, if

Sea thrift (Armeria maritime*) and yellow kidney vetch* (Anthyllis vulneraria*) growing on a Devon cliff top.*

you can translate these names their meanings can be very helpful. Even if Latin was not a subject on your school timetable, many of the names are in fact quite familiar. Continental names, such as *africanus*, *asiaticus* and *europeus*, are too vague to be helpful. But more precise locations can be of use: *Nepeta sibirica* and *Iris sibirica* are all hardy enough to withstand Siberian conditions, while *Geranium himalayense* and *Euphorbia sikkimensis* come from the Himalayas and Sikkim in the Himalayan foothills. It's worth checking the height at which they occur naturally to see if their seed might need a little chilling in order to germinate.

Often any one country has many different climatic conditions and defining the country of origin may still not be precise enough. Some species names, however, indicate the conditions that the plant prefers. *Centaurea montana* grows in the mountains, in Europe as it happens. The epithet '*palustris*' means marshy, so *Caltha palustris* grows in boggy ground. Its common name, marsh marigold, gives the game away. So its seedlings could dry out easily. And *Armeria maritima*, the sea thrift, grows in maritime areas, on steep, windy seaside cliffs, so it prefers well-draining soil in sun, as a result of which the seedlings could easily be overwatered. These and many more species names are both helpful and interesting.

IDENTIFYING PLANTS TO RAISE FROM SEED

Growing from seed is a long-winded procedure, so it is important to work out which plants will produce what sort of seedlings. Some exotic plants do not produce viable seed in this country, mostly because our summers are neither hot nor long enough. The pineapple broom (*Cytisus battandieri*), for example, sets seed only after a long, hot summer. Perhaps it will do so more often in the UK if the summers continue to get warmer.

Some plants, such as skimmias and hollies, mostly have separate male and female plants. If there is no male plant in the vicinity, the female will not produce berries, whereas all primulas are either male- or female-dominant: they will self-pollinate if all else fails. Their respective reproductive parts

DOUBLE-FLOWERED PLANTS

Double primrose 'Val Horncastle'.

Many fully double-flowered plants, such as double primroses, have petals in place of the reproductive parts of their flowers. This makes them mostly sterile. Some doubles produce a little precious pollen which can be used to pollinate single flowers, resulting in a proportion of doubles. But many doubles have to be propagated by division.

In the past, in Victorian times in particular, double primroses were divided continuously to provide quantities of plants for fashionable spring bedding. As a consequence of this clonal division, the plants were never able to build up any genetic resistance to viruses as they might have done had they been seed-raised. By the mid-twentieth century, double primroses had become little more than sickly rarities. In recent years, however, double primroses have been micropropagated. The process has cleaned out the viruses and made them available once again through nurseries and garden centres.

Pin-eyed primula.

are positioned more prominently. Female-dominant primulas are 'pin-eyed': the central stigma looks like the head of a pin. Male-dominant primulas are 'thrum-eyed': their anthers are set in a circular pattern like a thrum or skein of wool. They were named by the artisan spinners and weavers of the early nineteenth century who bred them for exhibition.

And some plants just seem to be sterile. Neither the lovely airy *Stipa gigantea*, nor the darling of every Chelsea Flower Show, *Cirsium rivulare* 'Atropurpureum', sets viable seed.

The general rule, however, is that seedlings of any plant with two names – a genus and a species, such as *Verbena* (genus name) *bonariensis* (species name) – will be more or less the same as each other,

Thrum-eyed primula.

Sterile seeds of Cirsium rivulare *'Atropurpureum'.*

Papaver orientale *'Coralie' discovered in a Somerset garden.*

but not identical. The seedlings of any plant with three names – a genus, a species, and a cultivar name, such as *Papaver* (genus) *orientale* (species) 'Patty's Plum' (cultivar name) – will, by definition, be different from the parent and from each other. That is, seedlings are not, and cannot be named *Papaver orientale* 'Patty's Plum'. In order to reproduce that particular plant it is necessary to use a form of clonal propagation, such as division or root cuttings. But seed from these individuals could be used to select from and name a new cultivar plant: *Papaver orientale* 'Lucky Break', perhaps.

Or seed could be collected from lots of different-coloured *Papaver orientale* to produce a deliberate mix of coloured seedlings to populate a sunny border. Usually there will be a predominance of reds and oranges, so in order to ensure that *P. orientale* 'Patty's Plum' does not throw seedlings too close

to the parent plant for comfort, it is important to cut off those beautiful seed heads before they ripen.

Some plants, such as aquilegias, do not lend themselves to clonal propagation, so they are generally seed-raised from isolated plants, then grown on in pots to the flowering stage to check the flower colour before planting out. Aquilegias are notoriously promiscuous, so this is an essential stage of the process if you want flowers of a particular colour or habit.

Annuals and biennials (that take two years to flower) can only be propagated by seed. Flower stem cuttings are unable to make roots and individual annual plants do not make crowns that can be split up. However, some plants, such as *Nicotiana*, the tobacco plants, are in fact tender perennials and could be propagated clonally if they were not so easy to grow from seed.

NAMED CULTIVARS COMING TRUE FROM SEED

For one reason or another, certain named cultivars will reproduce themselves almost identically from seed. There will be very few rogues. Although this is by no means a comprehensive list, it might prove useful:

- *Abutilon vitifolium var.* 'Album'
- *Alcea rosea* 'Nigra' (if self-pollinated)
- *Allium carinatum subsp. pulchellum f. album*
- *Aquilegia flabellata f.alba* (if self-pollinated)
- *Aquilegia vulgaris* 'Munstead White' (*syn. A.v.* 'Nivea') (if self-pollinated)
- *Aquilegia vulgaris* 'Nora Barlow' (if self-pollinated)
- *Borago officinalis* 'Alba'
- *Carex comans bronze form*
- *Daphne mezereum f.alba*
- *Gentiana asclepiadea var.alba*
- *Geranium pyrenaicum* 'Bill Wallis'
- *Geranium sylvaticum f.albiflorum*'
- *Hesperis matronalis var.albiflora*
- *Lathyrus latifolius* 'Albus'
- *Lathyrus vernus* 'Alboroseus'
- *Liatris spicata* 'Alba'
- *Lobelia* 'Compliment Scarlet'
- *Lobelia* 'Queen Victoria'
- *Lobelia siphilitica* 'Alba'
- *Lychnis flos-cuculi var. albiflora*
- *Lychnis viscaria* 'Alba'
- *Malva moschata f.alba*
- *Malva sylvestris* 'Brave Heart'
- *Milium effusum* 'Aureum'
- *Oenothera stricta* 'Sulphurea'
- *Salvia patens* 'Cambridge Blue'
- *Salvia patens* 'Oxford Blue'
- *Tropaeolum majus* 'Variegatum' and 'Alaska' (variegated nasturtiums)
- *Viola* 'Bowles' Black'

But, as in all things, there are exceptions. Life and living things are never that simple. Plants with the cultivar name 'Alba' (for example, *Geranium pratense* 'Alba') will produce a proportion of white-flowered seedlings. Although 'Alba' is written as a cultivar name, it only means that the flower is white and any white-flowered form could be called 'Alba'.

Aquilegia vulgaris.

BREEDING PLANTS

The technicalities of plant genetics can be so daunting to gardeners that they choose not to indulge in a bit of plant breeding. But anyone can have a go and by deliberately crossing known flowers the results are rewarding.

Cross-Pollination

Cross-pollinating plants within a species (for example, crossing *Papaver orientale* 'Patty's Plum' with *Papaver orientale* 'Prinz Eugen') is the most common and successful method of hybridization. Cross-pollinating plant species within a genus is less so. But there are plenty of examples: *Hydrangea* 'Preziosa' has been confirmed as a bi-specific cross between *Hydrangea serrata* and *Hydrangea macrophylla*. Its name should be written: *Hydrangea × hybrida* 'Preziosa'. The '×' denotes the bi-specific cross.

Leylandii conifers, the curse of late twentieth-century garden boundaries, are a much rarer thing: a bi-generic cross. Their botanical name is × *Cupressocyparis leylandii*. The '×' denoting the hybrid, this time between the two genera: *Cupressus* and *Chamaecyparis*. They are both within the botanical family *Cupressaceae*. Hybridizing genera sometimes gives rise to 'hybrid vigour', which is what has happened to those leylandii.

Cross-pollinating plants that belong to different botanical families belongs only in the realms of genetic manipulation: it does not happen in the garden or in the wild.

Hellebore hybrids.

Helleborus × ericsmithii is a three-way cross between H.niger and H. × sternii, which itself is a cross between H.argutifolius and H.lividus. It is commercially micropropagated.

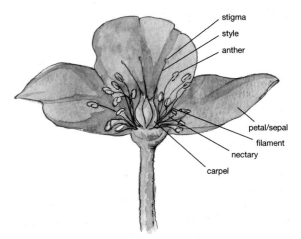

Reproductive parts of a hellebore flower.

Breeding from Seed

Breeding from seed can be very successful, but, according to how long a seedling takes to flower, the years can go by quickly, so it helps to have a goal and to bear in mind a few principles.

For the parents, choose healthy plants that display at least some of the features you would like to see. Good parents make good seedlings. Always cross the best with the best. The mother plant, the seed parent, should be vigorous and productive of seed. The father plant, the pollen parent, must display the features for which you are breeding. For example, if you want to breed oriental hellebores (*Helleborus × hybridus*) to produce flowers with red spots on a yellow ground, you would choose a spotty white mother and a yellow father. They don't sound a very prepossessing couple. But yellow oriental hellebores make very bad mothers. They are usually rather weak and produce little seed, so it is best to ensure that the pollen parent, the father, is as yellow as possible. Choose a well-spotted mother (spotting is genetically dominant), preferably with a white or cream ground colour. Green, pink and plum-coloured hellebores tend only to produce green, pink or plum seedlings. They are dominant colours; yellow and white are less dominant. As you see, it helps to have some experience of growing hellebores. Bees are the natural pollinators of hellebores, so the trick is to get to the seed parent (the mother) before the bees do.

Choose a half-closed bud and gently reflex back the petals to expose the stigma. In hellebores, the stigma has been found to be receptive to pollen before the flower opens fully. Using tweezers, pluck a group of stamens from the selected pollen parent (the father), making sure that the pollen is fluffy and ripe. Brush the stamens across the stigma. Close up the petals again. Loosely tie a length of nylon knitting yarn around the neck of the flower so that you can identify the hand-pollinated flower from the others. Label the plant with details of the parents. Ideally, repeat the exercise for three days running. With luck, the bees will not have sabotaged your work and the pollinated flowers will produce seed by the end of May or early June. Hellebore seed should be sown within a week or two, kept cool and shaded, and will germinate after the first frosts of winter.

When the first generation of seedlings comes into flower, pick the best plants that most closely exhibit yellow flowers with spots, then cross them with each other or with a parent. If there is only one seedling that fits the bill, fertilize it with its own pollen. This is called 'selfing'. Note, though, that too much 'selfing' reduces the vigour of the subsequent seedlings. Repeat the exercise one or more times; each generation of flowers will be better. But remember that it takes three years to flower a hellebore from seed. It's a long business. However, when you put a finger under the chin of a new flower and lift its face, the thrill is worth the long wait.

Helleborus × hybridus – *yellow, red central splash.*

PLANT BREEDERS' RIGHTS

When a particularly good cultivar has been bred and selected, the breeder will put on a form of copyright for plants called Plant Breeders' Rights. This permits the propagation of the plant only under licence. A capitation fee is paid to the breeder for every plant successfully produced. Propagation of the plant for sale commercially is not permitted without a licence. The licence reimburses the breeder for the expense of building up large numbers of the plant, usually by micropropagation, and for the publicity involved in launching the plant onto the market. Plant Breeders' Rights usually endure for twenty-five years.

SEED COLLECTION AND GERMINATION

Ideally, seed should be harvested on a dry, still day as soon as the seed pods have gone brown and are starting to split. Berried seed should be juicy and ripe. If the summer is relentlessly wet, the seed pods can be put in paper bags (marked with the name and date) and kept somewhere warm and dry for a few days. Then clear a large table and put down a clean sheet of plain paper. Tip out the contents of each paper bag in turn, sorting through the debris of dried pods and dead insects to find the hard, bright seeds. If the seed does not appear to be hard, it is possible that it is sterile, that is, it has not been fertilized and will not germinate. One way to test the seed is to sow a pinch of it on a sheet or two of moistened kitchen towel. Keep it warm and damp and see if it germinates within a week – or not.

Some seed can be collected a little early and kept to ripen in a paper bag. For example, hellebore seed will turn from stained ivory to ripe black whether it is attached to the plant or not. But not all seed pods will ripen once they are detached from the plant and it can be difficult to catch the seed at precisely the right time. Hellebores, notoriously, release their seed rather suddenly, early in the morning when only birds, mice and slugs are awake. So if you have missed the early warning signs of darkening seeds and failed to pick the seed pods a few days earlier, it's too late. However, it is possible to buy or make little drawstring muslin bags to pop over

*Ripe seed pods of the bladder senna (*Colutea arborescens*).*

Bags popped over ripening hellebore seed pods.

the ripening pods so that the seed is contained within the bag ready for collection. These are especially useful for those exploding geranium seed pods, too.

Seed Storage

Store the seed that does not have a short viability in a small paper envelope, marked with its full name and the date of its collection. Put the envelope into a sealed plastic box (a cleaned ice-cream container will do), then put the box in the bottom of your fridge. This will keep the seed at an even temperature of about 5°C (41°F), with the moisture content of the seed staying the same.

Seed with a Short Viability

Some seed has a very short storage life: it needs to be sown immediately, or at least within two or three weeks. Plump, succulent seeds, such as chestnuts, citrus or acorns, will die if they are dried out, so must be sown immediately. In the wild, they usually germinate immediately. This means that citrus seed would need to be sown in an entirely frost-free environment from the outset.

Not only hellebores, but primulas, cyclamen and pulsatillas also need to be sown fresh. Their seed is not fully mature when it is shed, so although these seeds will not germinate straight away, they need to experience the conditions they would in nature in order to finish ripening.

If the seed is unknown, it is worth dividing its number in two. Sow the first half immediately and the remainder can be stored until the spring.

Dormancy

Plants have developed all sorts of strategies to deal with climate conditions that do not favour vulnerable seedlings. Becoming dormant is the chief method of preventing seeds from germinating in adverse conditions and waiting for a change of season. In hot countries where there is a summer drought, annual plants predominate. They germinate, flower and set seed before the ground becomes scorched by the sun. Once the autumn rains return, the seeds germinate and the plants start their short life cycle again. Those perennial plants that do survive such conditions have developed different forms of protection against the sun, while their seed also is summer-dormant.

In high, mountainous regions, snow covers plants and their seeds like a duvet, maintaining a cool, even temperature. When the snow melts, the seeds are ready to germinate into warming soil moistened by the snowmelt and, significantly, when the winter cold will not return. The seasons are well-defined. The maritime climate of the UK brings fluctuating winter temperatures that can change from warm to cold, and back to warm again, in the space of a week.

Heat-Induced Dormancy

Anyone who has tried to grow a row of lettuces in a hot summer has come across this type of dormancy. The first spring-sown lettuce seedlings pop up with abandon to produce a glut. Then when at last those lettuces have all been eaten or gone to seed, the next sowing in mid-summer produces half-a-dozen limp specimens that never taste as good as those early ones. Most of the seed has become dormant with the hot weather. So, if there's a heatwave, sow the seed in a tray, water and drain it, then pop it in a plastic bag and put the whole lot into the fridge for at least a week until our typical English summer has expired in a thunderstorm. Or put the seed packet into the fridge and make a further attempt during a cooler week. That should be more successful.

Delphiniums and primulas also suffer from heat-induced dormancy. It follows, therefore, that their seed should be started off outdoors in early spring and not in a greenhouse. Even in spring, a greenhouse can experience soaring midday temperatures: 25°C (77°F) will initiate heat dormancy.

Packets of seed of Mediterranean plants, such as lavenders, rosemary or thyme or any seed from hot, arid, but not tropical, parts of the world, must be stored dry in summer, no matter where. Sowing this sort of seed as soon as it is ripe into a tray of compost and watering it regularly will result in the seed rotting before it can germinate. It is not what it would experience in the wild. In Britain, it needs to be sown in the spring when the temperatures are rising. In the wild, in Mediterranean regions, it would experience a summer drought and then germinate with the autumn rains and grow on during a very mild winter with higher light levels than in the UK.

Seed from tropical parts of the world should germinate at any time of year providing they are sown with bottom heat and kept at the correct temperature. However, common sense would suggest sowing in spring.

Stratification

The seeds of plants that come from mountainous regions, such as the Alps or the Himalayas, unsurprisingly, will not germinate before they have experienced a period of cold. In the autumn, this type of seed contains high levels of abscissic acid which prevents germination. This is dispersed when the temperature goes below 5°C (41°F), so after a long, cold period the abscissic acid will have gone and

the seed will then be able to germinate. Stratifying or exposing this seed to cold or even freezing temperatures, sometimes repeatedly, will imitate one or more winters.

Each seed has its own recipe: different lengths of hot and cold periods, different temperatures by day and night, temperatures below 0°C (32°F), and so on. However, most seeds that need chilling before they will germinate can be sown as soon as they are ripe into seed trays, then those trays watered and left outside to experience periods of frost before starting into growth. Such seeds need watering well so that they are fully imbibed with moisture before the temperature freezes. Although British winters vary in their temperature range, there are normally enough sub-zero nights to stratify most seed.

Often plants with hard, shiny seeds, such as aquilegia, dictamnus, ranunculus, saxifrage, thalictrum, trollius and tiarella, germinate better this way. However, it is necessary to protect the seed trays from birds with a net-covered frame, from mice with traps and from slugs with pubs (or pellets, if they are teetotal).

If such seed is not fresh and has been stored at room temperature, in the garden centre for example, there is a trick to try before giving up. Place a piece of kitchen paper in the bottom of a sealable plastic box, moisten it, then scatter the seed on top. Seal the box and allow the seed to imbibe the moisture overnight. Then put the box in the freezer for a week before sowing. Repeat the imbibing, freezing

Rhododendron arborea *flowering in the Himalayas.*

and defrosting procedure for every year of the age of the seed. It is particularly effective with old primula seed that is notoriously reluctant to germinate after storage, or if it has been purchased. Commercial seed is usually at least eighteen months old. It has to be collected, cleaned, packaged and distributed to the garden centre before you, the gardener, buys it and sows it.

Seed Chipping

Some seeds, members of the pea family in particular, have especially hard coats. (The many members of the pea family can be recognized by their distinctive lipped flowers.) Rubbing the seed between two sheets of sandpaper is the old method of weakening the hard coating, but it has been found that an overnight soak in a saucer of water is just as successful – and there is no risk of damaging the inner layers of the seed with over-enthusiasm.

Light and Oxygen

Some seeds need light for germination. More exactly, they need light plus the higher levels of oxygen on the surface of the compost: the deeper below the surface, the lower the levels of oxygen. For this reason, field poppies, for example, only germinate when their seed is turned up to the surface with the plough.

As a general rule of thumb, finer seed, such as foxgloves and tobacco plants, should be sown on the surface of the compost and barely covered. Larger seed, such as peas, beans and nuts, should be buried three times as deep as the diameter. Of course, there are exceptions: for example, nigella (love-in-the-mist) and phacelia have small seeds but they germinate better if they are well covered.

Delayed Germination

Some seed will naturally take more than one season to germinate. Beech trees, for example produce gluts of beech-mast every two or three years. Some of it germinates immediately; some a year later; and a little will not germinate for several years. The beech is keeping its options open: banking on at least one good spring in three or four.

Hypogeal Germination

Some seed (peonies are the classic example) have hypogeal germination. That is, only a root germinates from the seed during its first spring. The leaf shoot will usually appear the following spring (so long as the pot has not been tipped out in exasperation the year before by the impatient propagator).

The moral is to keep pots of unfamiliar seed for at least two years before giving up, weeding those pots with great care in the meantime.

Warmth

Most seed in the UK will not germinate before the soil temperature reaches 10°C (50°F), but many plants from warmer countries or tropical zones need a higher soil temperature. Their seed should be sown in a propagator with basal heat governed by a thermostat set at the correct temperature. Most seed merchants will give an indication of that temperature on the packet.

However, the majority of seed germinates readily without any special treatment once the soil conditions are right: that is, that there is enough moisture, warmth and oxygen present. So, with unknown seed, divide the amount in two. Sow half outdoors straight away to experience a cold period; keep the other half in a paper envelope in a sealed box, store it in the fridge, then sow it in the spring on the windowsill or in a frost-free greenhouse.

Peonia rockii.

SOWING THE SEED

One important principle of sowing seed is hygiene. Ideally, pots and seed trays should be newly bought, but the temptation to reuse existing containers is great. Providing they are thoroughly cleaned, the loss of seedlings will be minimal. It is quite possible that a healthy crop of hairy bittercress will emerge from tiny seed lodged in the crevices of uncleaned pots and trays, but the sown seed will germinate in the compost in the middle of the pot. If you only have a small amount of precious seed and no reserves, always use a newly bought container to sow it in.

There are all sorts of pots and trays available at garden centres nowadays, but the shapes and sizes you choose should be dictated by the plants you are growing. Hellebores, for example, have large roots. Even at the seedling stage they will plunge downwards seeking space. So their seed should be sown in deep pots to give them plenty of room to develop.

Tobacco plants (*Nicotiana*) have very fine seed that produces tiny seedlings, but they grow on very fast. A small, shallow seed tray would suit them, provided they are pricked out and potted up quickly and frequently.

Some seed hates disturbance. Poppy seed of any description is best sown into plug trays where each whole plantlet can be popped out without disturbing its roots and potted on or planted out. Poppies need to be a good size before they can face down the breakfasting slugs.

When to Sow

Too much warmth and not enough light will make young plants 'leggy'. That is, they will have long gaps between the leaf joints (internodes) and be susceptible to fungal disease. This is why it is essential not to sow too early: the levels of daylight are too weak in the UK until early March.

But there are, as ever, exceptions. For instance, gardeners tend to expect their pelargoniums to start flowering by June at the latest. Those pelargoniums that are raised from seed rather than as cuttings need therefore to be started off very early in the year (in late December or January) in a heated propagator. If sowing is left until March or April they will not

---

SETTING SEED IN WALLS

Old walls in old gardens are invariably filled with valerian, campanulas or *Erigeron karvinskianus* that have sown themselves into the cracks. Achieving this romantic look is easy. In February or March, take a pinch of seed and roll it into a little ball of wet soil. If your soil is so sandy that it does not stick together when wet, use a little John Innes No. 1 compost. Then, using your thumb, squeeze the mud-and-seed-pie well into the cracks. The seeds should germinate in the spring.

Campanula poscharskyana *and* Erigeron karvinskianus *growing out of a drystone wall.*

---

flower until the end of the summer. It is therefore essential to raise them in as much light as possible to prevent them from getting leggy.

Otherwise, start the general seed-sowing process with hardy annuals and early salad crops. Then when they have moved on, use the space to sow half-hardy annuals and vegetables. And finally, once all the early risers have left home, but before the summer has heated up, sow biennials followed by perennials.

Seed Composts

It is very important always to use a proprietary make of compost rather than sieved garden soil as our grandfathers did. They had no alternative, but they almost certainly achieved poorer rates of germination and those seedlings that did appear had to fight it out with a crop of very well brought-up weeds.

Multi-purpose compost.

Nowadays, proprietary seed composts are either loam-based – a John Innes mix – or you can use All-Purpose mixes based on peat or a peat substitute. Modern seed compost is sterile, that is, it should contain no weed seedlings, nor fungal spores nor eggs of insect pests. It is a mixture that drains well, while at the same time retaining enough moisture. In addition, the water can penetrate the compost when it dries out.

John Innes seed compost contains the correct amounts of nutrients for the seedlings before they are potted into a stronger mixture. All-Purpose mixes have rather more nutrients than is strictly necessary for raising seeds, but the compost remaining in the bag can also be used for pricking out the seedlings and potting them up.

Bags of seed compost should be kept dry: cover any that are left outdoors with a sheet of plastic whether they have been opened or not. A bag of seed compost should be used within a week or two of opening. Once moisture gets into the bag, the nutrients will be washed out and weed seeds and fungal spores can enter. Sciarid flies, in particular, lay eggs into moist, warm compost so that their larvae will hatch in time for their food to be supplied in the form of succulent seedlings.

Method

Fill the container loosely to the brim with seed compost, then take another identical container and press it down fairly firmly on the surface of the fluffy compost without compressing all the air out of it. The compost needs to have a flat surface just 1cm (⅓in) below the rim. Take a pinch of seed with thumb and forefinger and sprinkle it lightly all over the surface. Some people like to cut off the corner of the seed packet and tip it up; others cup the seed in their hands. Whatever method works best, the important point is that the seed should not be too thickly sown. Thickets of seedlings soon fall down, prey to damping-off fungus due to poor air circulation (*see* the section on Pests and Diseases in Part 3).

Cover the compost and seeds with a layer of horticultural grit, sharp sand, perlite or vermiculite. Horticultural grit is washed river grit or sand. Builders' sand is unsuitable because it contains too many salts, which will draw the moisture out of the seed. Perlite and vermiculite are very light, dry substances. They should be moistened before use.

Then label the container with the name and date and stand it in a tray of water to soak up the moisture from below. Watering with a can often puddles the seed into the centre of the container or even washes it out over the edges.

If the seed is sown in spring, place it on a shady windowsill, in a cold frame, or on a greenhouse bench. Avoid anywhere that gets too sunny, or the emerging seedlings will frazzle.

Some people place a sheet of glass on top of the seed tray and cover that with newspaper; some use cling film and newspaper. Provided the seed is sown at the correct depth and not placed in the sun, this should not be necessary. The risk when the compost surface is covered, and so not visible, is that the seed

Hellebore seed.

Cover the seed with horticultural grit and label.

will germinate very quickly while your back is turned, growing tall, thin and useless before you notice.

If the seed is vulnerable to heat-induced dormancy, place the seed tray outside and invert a clean, matching seed tray over the top, holding it down with a stone. The rain will get in through the drainage holes of the upper tray, but will not wash away the seeds. Inspect the tray every day, removing the upper tray as soon as germination occurs.

If the seed needs warmth to germinate, there are various makes of propagators on the market (*see* the section on Tools and Equipment in Part 3). If possible, choose one with a thermostat to set and regulate the temperature: some seeds germinate and fry up in a very short space of time.

If the seed is sown in summer, place the moistened seed container somewhere shady where you will remember to keep it watered. Protect any seed

trays placed outdoors from birds by covering the tray with a wooden frame fixed with fine netting; from mice with traps; and from slugs in whatever way you favour.

All seed varies in the time it takes to germinate. If it is old seed or bought seed, sow much more than you think you'll need, but not too thickly. Fresh seed, or home-collected seed that has been correctly stored and, if necessary, given the correct treatment, should germinate better. One way to test the viability of any stored seed is to sow a tiny pinch on a moistened kitchen towel in a tray. Put cling film over the top and place it on a sunny windowsill. This will force the germination, although the resultant seedlings will be useless.

Trays of seedlings such as hellebores that germinate after the process of stratification or have emerged after delayed germination should be placed

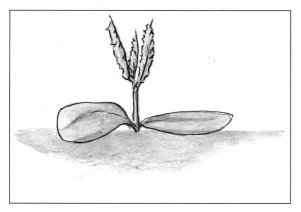

Seedling with cotyledons and true leaves appearing.

immediately into the protection of a cold frame or a greenhouse. Quite often, a sudden freezing spell can set back such seedlings considerably, even if they are frost-hardy when mature. Once they have produced true leaves they can be pricked out or potted up and placed either outside in a cold frame or kept in the greenhouse. But as soon as the majority of the seed has produced seedlings with true leaves that resemble the plant's leaves, rather than its seed leaves (the cotyledons, which appear first), it is time to move on to the next step.

AFTERCARE AND MAINTENANCE

In many ways, this subject is the one that should be considered first, well before opening that first packet of seed and filling every available space with pots and trays. This is because it is space, or the lack of it, which dictates every move that follows. It's tempting to give a chance of life to every last seedling that has germinated. But a quick glance around where you intend putting them at the next stage, and then at every subsequent stage, should harden the heart. As a rule of thumb, allow for a loss of 10 per cent in the number of plants at each stage of potting and planting, then work the sums out to decide on how many seedlings to keep. And the remainder? Throw them on the compost heap. It only takes a few seconds and you'll all feel better for the decision.

Pricking Out

Once a seed has germinated it produces seed leaves, or cotyledons, that act as a store of nutrients for the seedling until it has made enough root to survive. When the seedling has produced its true leaves, that

---

PROPAGATING LILIES FROM SEED

Many lilies suffer from viruses; growing them from seed prevents the transmission of viruses in lilies. Collect the seeds when they are ripe. You can tell if they are viable by holding each papery seed up to the light and looking for a line. If there is no line, the seed is infertile.

It can also be fun to do a bit of lily breeding. If you want to try your hand, it is simpler to use parents from within the same type of lily. There are three basic groups: the Asiatic hybrids; Trumpet hybrids and species; and the Turk's cap lilies. *Lilium pumilum*, *L. davidii*, *L. henryi* and *L. longiflorum* germinate easily and quickly in their first spring after sowing. This is called epigeal germination.

The Western American and oriental species and hybrids and the Turk's caps and their hybrids take a year longer to germinate naturally. During the first spring after sowing, the seed roots will germinate underground. Nothing will be visible on top until the following spring when the shoot pushes up through the soil (hypogeal germination).

However, it is quite easy to trick these hypogeal seeds into believing that two winters have passed. Sow the seed of hypogeal varieties in September in the gentle warmth of a frost-free greenhouse. After a minimum of six weeks, when the weather gets colder move them outside for a cold spell for another six weeks. Then bring them back into a warm environment (a heated greenhouse or a kitchen windowsill) until they start to shoot. Transfer them back to the frost-free greenhouse and prick out the growing bulbs two or three to a 7cm (3½in) pot. Don't tip out the seed tray, however. Often, hypogeal seeds take more than two winters to germinate. The bulbils will need to be grown on for at least four or five years before they are mature enough to flower. Pot them on each spring. Epigeal-germinating lilies will germinate the following spring after sowing. They have no need of any treatment. (To divide lily bulbs, *see* Part 2, Clonal Propagation.)

is, leaves that resemble the parent plant, it is time either to prick out or pot up into fresh compost that contains more nutrients. The potential size of the plant dictates whether to prick out small seedlings into trays.

Fill the container with the appropriate potting compost very loosely to the rim. It will bed down when the seedlings have been transplanted and watered in. Using an old kitchen fork, gently remove the seedling from the seed tray, holding it by a leaf or a cotyledon (seed leaf). If you pull off a cotyledon at this stage, the little plant is less damaged than if a true leaf has been lost. However, if you have damaged the seedling and there are plenty of others, throw it away. Never hold a seedling by its stem: the merest touch will bruise the cells in the stem and it will keel over and die in days.

Dibble the small seedlings into a standard size tray of potting compost using the end of a pencil or a thin stick. Make a grid pattern in the tray: 4–5 rows of most seedlings should allow enough room for a few weeks' growth.

Big seedlings such as peonies should be planted into 7cm (2¾in) pots.

Always choose to prick out the strongest little plants with the largest root systems and short gaps between the sets of leaves (the internodes). However, in the case of stocks (*Matthiola incana*) it is the smaller seedlings that are often the ones with double flowers. Check the seedlings for any signs of pests and disease. If they are closely packed together in the seed tray and their stems are grey where they meet the compost; or patches of them have collapsed, they are suffering from the fungal

Primula seedlings ready to be pricked out.

Gently remove the seedling from the tray.

Hold the seedling by the seed leaf.

The weight of the root ball supported by the fork.

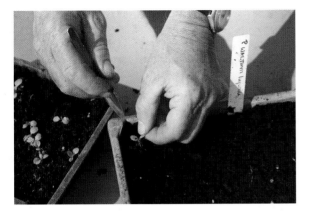

Plant the seedling in the pricking-out tray.

Gently firm the compost around the seedling.

A tray of twenty primula seedlings pricked out . . .

. . . and watered-in thoroughly.

Peony seedlings that have made leaves after two years' germination.

Tip out the pot of seedlings.

After two years, the pot may need squeezing.

Peony seedlings make deep roots.

Handle the seedlings carefully.

Gently prise the seedlings apart.

Separate the roots.

Remove the liverwort that has settled on the surface without damaging the stems.

Tease it off carefully.

Tip up a pot and half-fill it with compost. (The pea-like seeds are still visible.)

Hold the seedling by its leaf.

disease called 'damping off'. You will need either to start afresh and sow them all over again, or to choose isolated seedlings well away from any sicklings. Once you have pricked them out, water them in with a fungicide and keep a close eye on them. Greenfly are also fairly obvious: before they become bloated and green, they are tiny and white. It's easy to confuse young greenflies with whiteflies, but these fly off when they are disturbed, which greenfly do not. (Also, an infestation of whiteflies is unusual on young seedlings.) If the seedlings are infested, either start again or choose the healthiest seedlings that seem undamaged. Then spray them regularly with an aphicide to kill off the greenfly. (*See* the section on Pests and Diseases in Part 3 for more details.)

Fill up the pot.

Bigger seedlings, or those that resent root disturbance, should be put into a plug tray. Smaller, less vigorous seedlings make a denser grid if you want that many. Use half-trays if you do not. Sometimes very small seedlings, such as tobacco plants, trailing lobelia or fine grasses, for example, can be bunched together in groups of five or six. It will be necessary to water them in with a fungicide.

Hellebore seedlings that arise from hand-pollinated seed sometimes betray their colour in the leaves and stems. So from the seedling candidates for our potentially yellow hellebores with red centres, discard any that have dark stems. There is a strong possibility that they would have dark flowers. Hellebores have such large root systems from the outset that they also need to be pricked out into 7cm (2¾in) pots.

If the seedlings are big enough, nip out their tips with finger and thumb. Otherwise, this operation can be done when they have grown to the next stage. Then finally, when they have been watered in with a fine rose on the watering can, transfer the label from the seed tray and mark the date. Then that game of solitaire begins: finding somewhere to put the trays of eager little seedlings. Each must have enough light and most need protection from the frost.

Those seedlings that have germinated in a heated propagator should be first weaned out of the propagator and into a cooler environment that is still frost-free before being pricked out. Thereafter they

Select the paler seedlings.

Selected seedlings potted up.

A pot of hand-pollinated yellow/red-spotted hellebore seedlings.

Place the seedlings in a cold frame.

will need to be kept in a frost-free environment until they are hardened off and put outside after all danger of frost has passed.

Tough little seedlings that have germinated out-doors in a cold frame can be put back into the cold frame again after they have been pricked out.

Roguing

The white-flowered form of a species often bears the cultivar name 'Alba' or *var. alba*, indicating its colour. It is the albino form of the species but in all other respects it is an ordinary seedling. If these albinos are grown separately and away from their coloured brothers they will mostly produce white seedlings. The pollinating insects will in the main

Digitalis purpurea *'Alba'*.

have collected pollen and fertilized the flowers within that stand of plants. However, the laws of genetics will assert themselves and a small propor-tion of seedlings will turn out to have the natural-coloured flowers. Often, these coloured seedlings can be distinguished from the albinos by the colour of the leaves or veins.

In white-flowered foxgloves (*Digitalis purpurea var. alba*), for example, the albino seedlings have white veins. Those with purple-pink veins will produce the usual mauve flowers. So it is easy to sort them out as seedlings and throw away the unwanted mauve ones with mauve veins. This is called roguing: getting rid of the rogues.

Variegated plants that are known to produce variegation from seed, such as aquilegia, can also be rogued as soon as the true leaves emerge with or without the variegation. Occasionally, as is the case with honesty (*Lunaria annua*), this form of variegation takes a little time to appear, so if all the seedlings are green don't despair. Wait a little while; some may yet become variegated.

Less certain, but still helpful, is roguing for dark-coloured flowers. Oriental hellebores with dark plum or black flowers usually, but by no means always, exhibit black mottled stems and a dark edge to their leaves. Pale-flowered forms tend to have pale stems and leaves. But it is only a tendency and therefore only useful if there are more seedlings than you want.

Beware, however, of named white cultivars. *Brunnera macrophylla* 'Dawson's White' may or may not produce white seedlings. In any case, for a plant to be called *B. macrophylla* 'Dawson's White' it would need to be clonally propagated because it has a cul-tivar name. The seedlings that do bear white flowers would be *Brunnera macrophylla var. alba*.

Growing On

Once the pricked-out seedlings have grown suffi-ciently, nip out the growing tip with finger and thumbnail. This will make the young plants stockier and bushier. It is especially important with annuals, which otherwise would run up to flower on a single stem, set seed and die, in all too short a time. Large trays of small seedlings can be shorn with a pair of sharp secateurs if nipping them out is too fiddly.

Propagating Ferns from Spores

There are three basic methods of propagating ferns: by division in early spring; by growing on fernlets; and by cultivating spores. The first two methods are described in Part 2, Clonal Propagation. The latter method is one of the most fascinating forms of propagation in the plant world. It is not difficult; it merely demands scrupulous cleanliness. And patience.

Ferns produce spores at maturity on the underside of their leaves in countless billions. They are ripe when they can be dispersed into dense clouds with a touch of the leaf. Collect them by cutting the spore-bearing fronds and placing them on a plain sheet of paper, then covering that with a piece of blotting paper or newspaper to prevent the spores from blowing away. Leave them for a few days and then carefully lift off the blotting paper and the leaf. Pick out the leaf debris, or tip up the paper and the larger chaff will drop off with a light tap. Fold the paper down the middle and tip the spores into a sterile container (a small plastic box with a lid is ideal). Containers can be sterilized with baby-bottle sterilizing solution.

It is possible to store spores of most varieties of ferns in the box for quite a long time in the fridge until they are required, with the exception of the royal ferns, *Osmunda regalis*, which do need to be sown immediately.

Use a mix of moss peat and coarse sand, or compost specially formulated for African violets if it's available. Sterilize the mix either by putting it in a pressure cooker or a microwave for a few minutes; or in a very low oven (250°F/130°C/gas mark ½) for an hour. Put a shallow layer (about 1cm/⅓in deep) in the bottom of a sterilized pot and cover it with a layer of coarse, sterilized grit, then dampen it with sterilized water.

Sprinkle the surface of the grit with the spores, keeping them thinly and evenly distributed. Cover the pot with cling film secured with a rubber band and stand it in a saucer of sterilized water to imbibe.

Germination is erratic, variable and slow among the genera, but when it occurs it is quite different from seed germination. The first stage is the germination of the prothallia as flat, green heart shapes. These can be sprayed gently to encourage

Fern fronds.

the spermatozoids to swim to them and fertilize the prothallia. Then the minute young ferns start to grow: a hand lens provides a fascinating glimpse of the process.

Once the mini-ferns are getting a bit congested, gently lift them and transplant them in clumps into trays, and then again into small 5cm (2in) pots. Keep them moist at all times and clearly labelled. They are impossible to identify in the early stages. At this point, an application of fungicide and a reduction of moisture levels will help to prevent damping-off, which is both common and discouraging. The young plants should then be ready to plant out after about two years.

Potting On

As the seedlings fill their pricking-out trays, plugs or first pots, their roots will start to emerge from the drainage holes at the bottom. They then need potting on into fresh compost to provide them with the extra nutrients that will maintain their growth. It might seem logical to put them into larger containers from the beginning, but there are all sorts of hazards involved in this apparent short cut. Most importantly, they can get overwatered. The vacant compost acts like a sponge, with the result that all that wet rots the roots. Some plants' roots seek the walls of the pot, leaving wet compost directly under the main stem, rotting the base of the stem. Also, the nutrients in that vacant compost will simply wash away. It is far better that the plants' roots fill the compost, so using up all the nutrients, and then they can be potted on again into fresh compost.

Trays of pricked-out seedlings are now robust enough to be tipped out onto a bench and each little

plant teased gently apart from its neighbours. Take care not to pull the top growth away from the root ball.

Put a little fresh compost into the base of a small pot. Then, holding the plant by a leaf at the correct level, fill the pot with compost around the root ball and up to the rim, tapping it down on the bench to settle the compost. Alternatively, fill the pot very loosely with compost and push in your index finger to make a hole. Then drop the little plant's roots into the hole. Tap the pot and the compost will fall back in to fill up the pot. It might need a little extra compost, but make sure the finished level is just a little higher than the base of the plant's top growth: it will settle back down when watered. If the root ball is proud of the compost level it will dry out, while the top growth will be unstable and rocky.

Once the whole batch has been potted on, water the plants well to settle the compost around the roots. Use a fungicide in the water if the seedlings have been planted deeply, so as to prevent the stem from rotting where it makes contact with the compost. Replace the label on the batch and add the potting date. If you have any doubt about recognizing any of the plants as belonging to that batch, it might be wise to label them all separately. When it comes to planting them out, it can be infuriating to have forgotten which plant is which. Is it a blue cornflower or a pink one?

Seedlings in plugs or already in small pots can be put directly into a larger pot of fresh compost.

Seedlings of Salvia *'Forest Fire'.*

The tips nipped out.

Plug tray of Papaver commutatum *'Ladybird'.*

Plugs of P.c. *'Ladybird'.*

Potted plugs of P.c. *'Ladybird'.*

Tip the larger pot at an angle and put in a measure of compost: just a little less than half full should do. Holding the plantlet directly in the middle of the pot, set the pot back upright and the soil will fall back under the roots and around the plant. Still holding the plantlet upright with one hand, fill up the pot to the top. Tap it on the bench and the compost should settle down to about 1cm (⅓in) below the rim of the pot.

Hardening Off and Planting Out

Before planting out any young plants, they need slowly to get used to the higher light levels outside the greenhouse and, in spring, to the cooler night temperatures. This is called hardening off.

When the night-time frosts are over, the seedlings that have been raised inside a frost-free greenhouse should be moved outside during the day and returned inside at night for at least a week. During the second week leave them outside at night too, only bringing them in if the weather becomes extreme, such as very heavy rain or a very late frost.

During the early spring, prepare the ground for planting. Weed it thoroughly, fork in some garden compost or a light application of organic fertilizer, then rake it over. Check over the young plants for any signs of greenfly and spray them if necessary. Cut them back again with a pair of secateurs to encourage them to bush out, especially if they are a little tall and thin.

Full pots of Papaver commutatum *'Ladybird'.*

Roots appear through the drainage holes.

Roots fill the pot.

Papaver
commutatum
'Ladybird'
*with ox-eye
daisies.*

WATERING

Plants in pots will need watering every day during which there is no rain in summer. Light showers can be deceptive, however. If the rain is not sufficient for you to put up an umbrella or make the ground beneath the car wet, it is not enough to penetrate the surface of potted plants.

Water in the cool of the evening to prevent loss from evaporation and to allow the young plants to imbibe the moisture throughout the night. Hand-watering with a hose should be methodical. Water every pot up to the brim (which is why it is essential not to overfill a pot with compost at potting time). Allow a spray line to water for ten to fifteen minutes at a time. There is no need for more, even on very dry days: there is only so much water a pot and its compost can hold.

As autumn comes in, the potted plants outside will need watering less frequently, until by winter they mostly will not need watering at all, although watch out that evergreens in pots outside do not dry out on windy days. (Most evergreens are safer inside a cold greenhouse or frame in winter anyway.)

Unlike the garden, the plants in the greenhouse and cold frames will obviously need watering throughout the year. Give them a thorough watering, not a sprinkling. Little and often leads to the roots coming to the surface and drying out even faster. Watering should not become a habit, especially in the winter. It is better to check the surface of the compost and water only when it becomes too dry. In summer, however, they will need watering regularly; probably every day. In very hot weather, spray over the floor of the greenhouse at midday to reduce the ambient temperature. The plants will compensate by needing less irrigation in the evening.

As the summer turns to autumn and winter the plants will need less water, until by December they will probably only need watering once a week. In winter, do the watering early in the morning to allow the sun and the ventilation to dry the foliage during the day. However, it is always better to keep plants on the dry side in winter. Too much moisture in winter makes near-dormant roots rot and brings on the dreaded fungal diseases.

As plants get leafier in spring they will again start to need increasingly more water. All those extra leaves are losing moisture from the plant at a much faster rate. They may even need watering twice a day if it is too soon to pot them on but the pots are full of roots. If the plants are potted into a soil-less compost, they will need more water than if they are potted into a John Innes loam-based one.

Watering cans.

Then plant them in the cool of the evening. Water them well. Protect them against slugs and snails in the usual way. And if you or your neighbours have cats, throw a net over the bed for a week or two while the plants get their roots firmly anchored. Cats will not risk catching their claws in nets. (But check the net daily for any trapped birds.)

Pests and Diseases of Seedlings

Pests and diseases are more common, more easily spread and more devastating within the enclosed warm spaces between seedlings. Good hygiene is the most important safeguard, as well as vigilance against any sign of pest attack. Seedlings are most at risk of the fungal rot commonly known as damping-off disease. A patch appears where newly emerged seedlings have keeled over and become black. It will spread within hours and soon demolish the whole crop.

To prevent seedlings from damping-off, sow the seed thinly to allow plenty of ventilation when they germinate, especially where the stalks meet the compost. Seedlings should also be given plenty of light to prevent them getting tall and etiolated, softer and more susceptible to disease. A chemical fungicide drench such as Cheshunt Compound can also be watered on when the seed is sown and again when the seedlings are pricked out.

Sciarid fly can be a problem when peat-based composts are used. The adults are black, about 4mm (0.16in) long and jump about on top of the containers. Their tiny white larvae are just visible on the surface of the compost and can attack the stems of seedlings. The easiest remedy is to clean off the top layer of compost and pot up the seedlings. A permethrin-based spray after the plants have been watered in is usually sufficient to effect a permanent cure. Sciarid flies rarely return once the pots have left the moist warmth of a greenhouse.

PART 2

Clonal Propagation

INTRODUCTION

The word 'clonal' can sound like something from the pages of a science-fiction novel. It is not. It simply means that each plant produced clonally, that is, by division or cuttings, contains precisely the same genetic mix as its parent. The genes have not been remixed as they are when raising plants from seed. The resulting plants will be completely identical to their parent and to each other. So, for example, divisions or root cuttings of *Papaver orientale* 'Patty's Plum' will all produce the same lovely crushed damson-coloured flowers and not vary in any way.

There are many different methods of clonal propagation, each of which has its own advantages and disadvantages. Each method suits a particular type of plant and each method is best carried out at a particular season: softwood cuttings of tender perennials in late summer; semi-ripe cuttings of evergreens in autumn and early winter; hardwood cuttings and division in winter; basal cuttings in spring; and grafting and budding at specific times throughout the year.

Choosing the correct material from the 'mother' plant is vital: semi-ripe and softwood cuttings from the current year's growth; root cuttings that are thick enough; divisions from the perimeter of the clump. There are many factors to take into consideration. And judging how many cuttings to take of a particular plant is not a precise science. It can depend on how easily a particular plant is to root; whether the cuttings are going to be kept in ideal conditions; as well as how many are needed in the first place.

Each of these topics will be covered in the separate sections below, followed by the methods of growing on and looking after newly rooted young plants; and finally, when to let them loose in the garden borders and enjoy the fruits of all that labour.

Papaver orientale *'Patty's Plum'*.

DICOTYLEDONOUS AND MONOCOTYLEDONOUS PLANTS

Flowering plants are divided into two groups: dicotyledonous and monocotyledonous. They are often referred to as dicots and monocots.

- Dicots include most trees, shrubs, roses and many perennials.
- Monocots include grasses, bamboos, cereals and some perennials, such as members of the lily and iris family, for example.
- Dicots have two seed leaves or cotyledons. Monocots have only one cotyledon.
- Dicots have branching veins in their leaves. Monocots have parallel veins.
- Dicots have flowers with different numbers of parts. Monocots have flower parts in multiples of three, such as irises.
- And, most importantly, dicots have a layer of cambium (*see* below) just beneath the skin or bark. Monocots have no cambium layer.

Dicotyledonous Papaver orientale 'Goliath' and aquilegias flowering with monocotyledonous Miscanthus sinensis 'Cosmopolitan'.

NODAL CUTTINGS

The node is the part of the stem of a plant where the leaf is attached. It usually contains a dormant bud that will become a side shoot.

The four different types of nodal cuttings – softwood, semi-ripe, hardwood and basal – are taken at different times of the year, but they are always from the current year's growth. Old, mature stems are usually too woody and more inclined to make flowers or side shoots than roots.

Plant Hormones

The process of photosynthesis provides the food for all green plants to grow and develop. But that process of growth and development is controlled by the plant hormones, the phytohormones. Phytohormones make the roots grow downwards and the shoots grow upwards (polarity). They cause shoots to grow towards or away from the light (tropism). They cause leaves to appear in spring rather than autumn, then drop off again in the autumn, not in spring; and so on. These phytohormones are affected by light, day length, and gravity, as well as interacting with each other in quite complex ways.

Auxins

A plant's ability to heal wounds and to root is controlled by one of a group of phytohormones called auxins. The auxin contained in hormone rooting powder is indoleacetic acid or IAA and it specifically controls root formation.

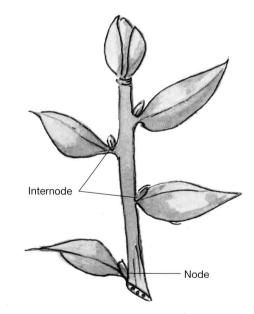

Internode

Node

Nodal cutting.

Gibberellins

Another group of phytohormones, the gibberellins, regulate the growth rate of plants. There is a concentration of gibberellins at the tip of every shoot, in particular the top-most shoot. They drive the upward growth of the plant and suppress the gibberellins in the side shoots lower down. This is called apical dominance. Christmas trees, for example, exhibit very strong apical dominance to provide a perfect perch for the Christmas angel. But most plants to a greater or lesser degree conform to this design of growth.

However, tall, thin plants are not usually required or desired. On the whole, we like our garden plants to be bushy and rounded. For this reason, among others, it is important to remove the growing tip, which is full of gibberellins, from the cutting. This releases the suppressed gibberellins in the lower side shoots and each will start to make its bid to be top dog: the plant will bush out.

Cuttings are taken just below the node for another very good reason. The stem contains vessels or tubes (xylem and phloem) that transport water, phytohormones and soluble nutrients up and down the plant. The point where a leaf and leaf bud, or a side shoot in the case of semi-ripe cuttings, joins the main stem is like a slip road off a motorway. Nutrients and phytohormones get congested and collect at this point like traffic held up at the junction. When you then cut below that node and seal the end with hormone rooting powder, those phytohormones have nowhere left to go. They collect and do what comes naturally to some of them: they make roots. The hormone rooting powder is there to add encouragement.

How Many Leaves to Leave?

The business of rooting all types of cuttings at any time of year is a question of balance between the effects of too much moisture and moisture loss. Too little moisture and the cutting flags and droops: it has no roots to take up the water it needs. Too much moisture in the atmosphere or the compost leads to rotting and fungal disease before the cutting has had a chance to root.

So it is a matter of judgment how much leaf to leave on the cutting when it is being prepared. The leaves are vital to the cutting while it produces new roots. They are the food factories of the plant. They produce sugars in the presence of light; they photosynthesize. On the other hand, the leaves draw the moisture out of the cutting and dry it out, especially in summer. So large-leaved cuttings that are taken in summer, such as hydrangea, should have their leaves reduced to achieve a better moisture balance.

Containing the cuttings within a plastic bag helps to prevent the leaves losing moisture in the movement of air and so conserve it in the leaves. On a larger scale, an enclosed mist unit is useful, especially for leafy cuttings taken in the summer (*see* the section on Tools and Equipment in Part 3). However, not all plants enjoy a lot of moisture. Drought-loving and silver plants will rot much more quickly in a damp atmosphere. For this reason, their cuttings are kept somewhere shady and cool but open to the air, rather than enclosed in a plastic bag or under mist.

Once the roots have appeared, the moisture in the compost is drawn up through the cutting and lost through its leaves. But there is still the risk of fungal disease entering the cutting where the leaves touch the side of the pot or each other.

Propagation Compost Mixes

There is no need to use all-purpose compost mixes for rooting cuttings. Not only are they an

Prepared hydrangea cutting with leaves reduced.

unnecessary expense (the cuttings cannot take up the nutrients), but their drainage is not sharp enough.

The compost for rooting cuttings, the prop mix, is very easy to make as and when it is needed. The basic mix comprises 50:50 peat/peat alternative to washed horticultural grit or sharp sand. Don't use builders' sand that is full of salts which draw the moisture out of the cuttings, so reversing the process of osmosis.

This basic mix can be adjusted to make it more free-draining by using a higher proportion of grit for drought-loving plants like lavender and pinks. The addition or substitution of propagation-grade, composted bark is good for evergreen cuttings that have to sit as cuttings throughout the winter and spring. Bark holds on to nutrients in the soil by ionization, whereas peat, grit and sand do not. A little slow-release fertilizer added to this mix will also feed evergreen cuttings once they have rooted but before they are potted.

SOFTWOOD CUTTINGS

Softwood cuttings are a useful way of making more plants to fill summer pots. They are a good introduction to the craft of taking cuttings. Non-hardy perennials such as pelargoniums, fuchsias, osteospermums and diascia are the easiest to propagate and success will whet your appetite for something trickier. They root quickly and easily, and they grow away fast. And, providing you have a cheap way of overwintering the cuttings, such as a cool windowsill or a frost-free porch, they will save the expense of buying new plants each spring.

But there are very many other plants that can be propagated by softwood cuttings, including hardy, deciduous shrubs, such as buddleia, weigela, philadelphus, ribes and rubus. These all produce non-flowering side shoots early in the summer, but which by the end of the year will have become too woody to root well.

Evergreen shrubs with grey leaves, such as lavenders, santolinas and artemisia, root better in summer than in winter. They are covered in tiny silver hairs to protect themselves from the sun in their native habitats, so they particularly dislike the dampness of a cold British greenhouse in winter. Many other evergreen shrubs that hail from Mediterranean-type climates such as California, South Africa, Australia and North Island, New Zealand, also dislike the winter wet. These too are more successfully rooted from young summer growth.

Alpines such as thymes, named gentians, saponaria and aubrietia, can also be easily rooted from their young side shoots.

Many herbaceous plants such as heleniums, penstemons and phlox that flower along leafy stalks are easy to propagate from softwood cuttings of their stems. Other herbaceous plants that produce flowering stems directly from the crown have no leaf nodes: Japanese anemones or oriental poppies, for example. They have to be propagated by another clonal method: division, basal cuttings or root cuttings.

Fuchsia cuttings growing on.

When to Take Softwood Cuttings

Softwood cuttings are taken from the growth that has been made during the spring and summer. The timing is in some cases critical; in others merely pragmatic. Non-hardy perennials, such as pelargoniums, fuchsias, osteospermums and diascia, root fast and grow away almost too quickly. Cuttings from these plants are best taken in late summer so that the resulting youngsters don't take up too much precious heated greenhouse or windowsill space over the winter.

Deciduous shrubs that flower before mid-summer, such as weigela, philadelphus, ribes and rubus, will push out side shoots after flowering to make growth to flower next year. As soon as these new side shoots reach the correct size they can be taken off with a heel. These will root easily and quickly at this time. Any later and the side shoots become too woody and far too long. Too soon and the cutting material is too soft and will wilt immediately it is cut off. Given the speed of growth early in the year, there is often only a fortnight's opportunity to take these cuttings.

Softwood cuttings of deciduous shrubs that flower after mid-summer, such as hydrangea and buddleia, should be taken as early in the summer as possible, as soon as the growth is firm enough. Ideally, they should be taken from non-flowering shoots, but they root so easily that just removing the flower bud is all that is needed. The later that the cuttings are taken, the more susceptible they are to the heat of those later summer months and all the problems that brings.

Silver-leaved woody plants tend to produce side shoots from the previous year's growth, reaching the correct length by about May or June in the UK. This material will root quickly and easily. The cuttings then should have made enough roots to be potted up by July or August and become strong young plants with woody stems that will survive the winter better.

Evergreen shrubs that come from a Mediterranean climate, such as cistus, ceanothus, myrtus and escallonia, are also easier to root in summer. They too need to have a healthy root system to withstand the damp winter atmosphere in the UK.

Gentiana *'Blue Silk'*.

Alpines and herbaceous plants root easily and quickly throughout the season, but it is wisest to take cuttings as soon as the growth is firm and long enough. They can then be potted up before the end of the summer, ready to plant out the following spring.

It is a general rule that the earlier in the summer softwood cuttings are taken, the more successful is their rooting. The resulting young plants will also have plenty of summer left in which to grow and make plenty of roots in order to survive the winter better and grow away the following spring.

Some plants, including clematis and certain cultivars of hardy geranium, need to make sufficient roots quickly enough to allow the plant to form a resting bud in the winter. The plant will then regrow the following spring. Consequently, these cuttings should be taken as early as possible in spring.

Method

Choose a cool, cloudy or even wet day to take cuttings, as they can flag and droop within minutes in the sun. Put the cutting material into a large plastic bag while you are collecting. And pop in a name label, especially if you are taking cuttings from different plants of the same genus.

If you cannot prepare the cuttings immediately, keep them in the loosely tied bag with the label and pop that in a domestic fridge. They can be stored for two or three days in the cool, constant temperature and humidity of a fridge.

Using a pair of sharpened, scissor-cut secateurs, remove a side shoot from the parent plant without disfiguring it. It should be between 10–15cm (4–6in) long, with at least two sets of leaves and a non-flowering tip. The gap between the nodes should be as short as possible. This gap is called the internode.

Check that there are no pests or fungal diseases present on the cutting and that the cutting is true to type. For example, if the plant is variegated, the

Remove a side shoot from Pelargonium *'Lady Plymouth'.*

Cutting below a node.

cutting material should also be variegated in the same way, such as with white or gold margins, splashes or zones. If the variegation is not already present in the cutting, the resultant offspring may not turn out to be variegated. If the plant is prostrate, that is, growing horizontally, take only cuttings of horizontal growth, not vertical shoots. The opposite is true in upright cuttings of tall, thin plants, botanically known as fastigiate plants. This mostly applies to evergreens and conifers, but also to ceanothus.

With a very sharp, straight-bladed knife make an oblique cut through the stem just below the node. The correct method is quite skilful, but it is worth practising. Bending the cutting over the blade, or putting the cutting down on the counter and pressing the blade through the stem just damages the structure of the stem. Imagine the xylem and phloem tubes that run up and down the stem to be like a bundle of drinking straws: they would just be squashed flat if you cut them in this way. An oblique angle on the cut also exposes more of the cambium layer where the roots form.

Avoid touching the base of the cutting. Your skin is greasy. A film of grease can inhibit rooting, contaminate the open wound and cause fungal infec-

> ### THE ROLE OF THE CAMBIUM LAYER IN ROOT FORMATION
>
> The plant hormones, the phytohormones that control root formation, are called indoleacetic acid, or IAA. They are concentrated in a thin layer just beneath the outer bark or skin, called the cambium layer. It is from this part of the stem that the young roots will emerge in a cutting.
>
> Cambium does not occur in monocotyledonous plants. Nor is it present in truly annual plants that germinate from seed, grow, flower and set their own seed within a single season. So cuttings cannot be taken from monocots or annuals. However, many plants that we as gardeners consider to be annuals are in fact merely fast-growing perennials that are not hardy in a British winter. These include many of our favourite container plants: pelargoniums, osteospermums and diascia, for example.

tion. Remove the leaves alongside the bottom node by cutting them down against the knife. Cutting them off from the top can damage the nodal bud,

The correct method is to make an oblique cut . . .

. . . drawing the knife away from the top of the cutting . . .

. . . exposing more of the cambium layer without squeezing the stems.

Ten prepared cuttings.

while pulling off the leaves often strips the skin off the cutting.

Remove the tip of the cutting. There are several reasons for this. Firstly, the tip is usually much softer than the rest of the cutting and could draw out the moisture or die back if it is left in place. Secondly, the tip often contains a tiny dormant flower bud, as a result of which the cutting could try to achieve motherhood rather than roots to prolong its genes. But, thirdly and most importantly, the tip contains all the phytohormones that make the shoot grow upwards and suppress the growth of the lower side shoots. As noted above, this is known as apical dominance. Most gardeners want bushy, rounded plants. Removing the tip allows the side shoots to develop. However, if the plant is to be a standard plant on a long stem, leave the tip in. It may be necessary to apply a fungicide to such cuttings and to ensure that the cutting never flags.

As you prepare the cuttings, lay them in an empty seed tray in groups of five, then ten. It's much easier to count them as you insert them (and to retrieve the number if you lose count).

If the cuttings have large leaves, such as hydrangeas and buddleias, cut the two remaining leaves in half. This reduces the amount of moisture that could be otherwise lost before the cutting has made any roots.

Peat/peat substitute and horticultural grit, clean pots, labels, secateurs, knife, marking pen and cuttings.

Peat/peat substitute mixed well with horticultural grit.

Dip the cutting into fresh hormone rooting powder.

Use a stick to dibble in the cutting.

Insert the cuttings around the edge of the pot.

How Many Cuttings to Take?

Most softwood cuttings root easily and the general rule of thumb to allow for a 10 per cent loss is about right. But some are more difficult than others, especially if they are taken a bit too late. *Prunus* (shrubby cherries), lilacs (*Syringa*) and mock orange (*Philadelphus*) can be very reluctant to root if the timing is wrong. To increase their rooting percentages it would be worth taking heeled cuttings. Other shrubs such as *Rubus spectabilis* 'Olympic Double' root well, but in practical terms the side shoots are more easily removed with a heel.

With a sharp pair of secateurs, remove a section of growth from the mother plant that has side shoots about 10cm (4in) long. Then holding the main stem in one hand and the base of the cutting where it joins the main stem in the other hand, pull downwards vertically. This should detach the cutting from the stem and include the thicker, swollen part of the stem around the junction. Alternatively, use your knife to remove the cutting with a heel, or a length of skin that comes away too. Cut away the surplus skin, leaving the swollen base entire with a little tail, the heel.

Inserting the Cuttings

Fill a thoroughly cleaned, preferably new, shallow pot or seed tray with cuttings compost. Put down the container smartly on the workbench to settle the compost just a little. Dip the end of the cuttings in fresh hormone rooting powder or gel and tap off the excess powder. There is no need to dip the

Rubus spectabilis 'Olympic Double'.

Use secateurs to remove the cutting material from Rubus spectabilis *'Olympic Double'.*

The cutting material in a plastic bag.

Detach the cutting with the swollen base of the stem.

The cutting comes away with a heel.

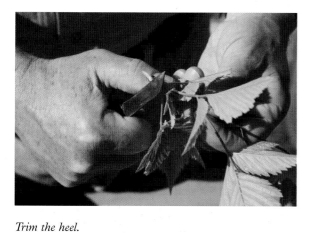

Trim the heel.

Cut off the lower leaves against the blade of the knife.

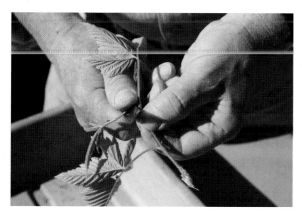

Remove the tip.

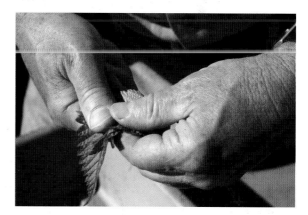

Bunch up the top growth.

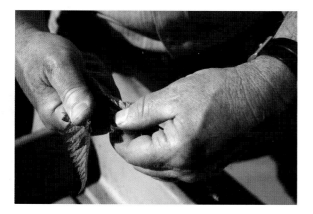

Cut the top growth in half.

Prepared cuttings ready for inserting.

HORMONE ROOTING POWDER OR GEL

Hormone rooting powder or gel contains the plant hormone IAA, indoleacetic acid. This auxin specifically controls root formation. As a live hormone, it should ideally be kept at a constant, cool temperature. A domestic fridge is ideal. However, it should be replaced after about six months as it has a limited storage life.

In addition to IAA, hormone rooting powder or gel contains a small amount of fungicide that helps prevent fungal disease entering through the open wound of the cutting. Sometimes it is barely necessary to use hormone rooting powder because a particular plant heals and roots so easily. But the counsel of perfection would urge its use anyway, just to benefit from the fungicide.

Dip the end of cuttings in hormone rooting powder.

cutting in water first to make the powder stick. This just makes a glutinous ball that gums up the base of the cutting.

Insert the cuttings around the edge of the pot, or, if they are quite small, in a grid pattern in a seed tray, making a hole with the end of a pencil or a dibber. Press the soil gently into contact with the buried stems. Make sure that the leaves are not touching the soil, the edge of the container or each other. Label each pot with the plant name, the number of cuttings and the date they were taken. In this way, you will gradually learn when and how many cuttings to take of a particular plant.

Water the cuttings in thoroughly with a fine rose on the watering can, then allow the container to drain for a few minutes. The finished soil level should be just a few millimetres below the top of the pot or tray. Too full and water will spill over the top; too little and the gap becomes deep enough to encourage fungal growth around the necks of the cuttings.

Put the container inside a big plastic bag. Blow into the bag with your breath, which will be rich in CO_2. Plants inhale CO_2 and exhale oxygen. This will also keep the sides of the bag from touching the cuttings. Finally, tie up the top of the bag tightly with twisty wire ties.

Alternatively, if the trays don't fit in bags you have to hand, there are propagating trays fitted with clear domes on the market that are ideal for trays of cuttings. These propagators do not need to have

Insert the cutting using a stake as a dibber.

Arrange the cuttings around the edge of the pot.

Water the cuttings in well.

bottom heat to root softwood cuttings (*see* the section on Tools and Equipment in Part 3).

Place the finished pot or the propagator somewhere cool and shady. Under the bench in the greenhouse is ideal, or on a cool windowsill, or in a shady porch. Open the plastic bag, or lift the lid on the propagator, every day or two to allow the condensation to drip down to the bottom. Remove any cuttings that have gone brown. They are a potential source of infection. Blow into the bag again and retie it, or close up the propagator.

The cuttings should have rooted, or not, in two to three weeks. They will look perkier: the buds of the side shoots will just be starting to swell and a very gentle feel of the leaf tip will meet with just a little resistance. Obviously it is important not to tug on the leaves and break any tiny hair-like roots beneath.

Aftercare

Once rooting has begun, open up the plastic bag or the vents on the propagator. After a few days remove the pot from the plastic bag, or take the dome off the propagator. Then, once the roots are just visible through the drainage holes of the pot or tray, gradually expose the cuttings to increasingly more light. At any sign of flagging or wilting, spray them over with water, then put them back in the bag or under the dome.

It is worth taking a moment to consider the nature of roots. They are made up of cells that are inflated like balloons. Their walls are so thin that moisture can penetrate them to enter the plant. The water in the soil is a weaker solution than the water in the plant and so the strong solution draws up the weak solution: the process of osmosis.

So, it follows that even touching those young roots will burst their little balloons and render them useless, requiring the cutting to make more roots. The bigger the root ball, the better, and the less any root damage matters. Any young plant will grow away faster from a larger root system.

Potting Composts

Having successfully rooted your cuttings or raised stocky little seedlings, you naturally want to give them a good upbringing. They deserve to be potted into the best compost for the job. Well-grown young-sters turn into healthy, vigorous plants, quickly. So put aside the old gardeners' ways of sifting garden soil and choose proprietary compost that has been manufactured for its purpose. This compost will have important properties:

- It will be sterile. That is, free from weed seeds, fungal spores and pest eggs.
- It will contain the correct mix of nutrients to maximize healthy growth and will state the proportions of major nutrients on the bag.
- It will be the correct pH for your plants: neutral in all-purpose compost and low in ericaceous compost for acid-loving plants.
- The air porosity will be balanced. Roots need oxygen as well as water between the soil particles.
- Some proprietary composts contain a chemical that deters vine weevils from laying their eggs.
- Some composts are peat-free, that is, they are made from a fibrous alternative. There are many on the market. Test them out first. Some mixes are very variable in quality, even between individual bags.
- John Innes Composts are loam-based. That is, they are composed of sterilized soil particles and a specific mix of nutrients suitable for three different stages of growth (J.I.1, J.I.2, J.I.3). They are less popular nowadays because they make potted plants heavy to lift, although this can be an advantage if you are growing top-heavy topiary in a pot. Loam chemically holds onto nutrients better and releases them slowly to the roots. It holds moisture well and re-wets more easily than peat-based compost. And vine weevils prefer peat to loam.

These composts can also be adjusted slightly for different sorts of plants by adding a little horticultural grit for plants that like poor, free-draining soil for instance.

It can be a little bewildering in the garden centre when faced with mountains of plastic bags of seemingly the same sort of compost. It's tempting simply to select the cheapest, but first try to work out why one bag of compost is cheaper than another. It's not always that the volume in the bag is less. Some composts contain sedge peat, which makes poor potting compost that drains badly, but is very cheap. (Grow bags are usually filled with sedge peat so as to hold the maximum amount of moisture for your tomatoes.)

Fertilizers

There is no need to work out a complicated chemical formulation and make your own fertilizers. There are plenty of organic and chemical fertilizer compounds on the market that are useful in different ways.

Liquid chemical fertilizers are immediately taken up by the plant through its roots or its leaves. So if you want to give any plant a quick fix to get it moving or flowering, this is the fastest method. Timing, therefore, is important: a flush of soft young growth in late spring followed by a night or three of frosts will seriously damage the whole plant. Liquid fertilizers high in nitrogen in particular should only be used once all danger of frost has passed. At the other end of summer, they should not be used after July so that any new growth has time to harden up for the winter.

Granular chemical fertilizers are also best applied in spring to promote quick growth and flowering. They also should not be used after the end of July.

Organic fertilizers are slower to break down and become available to the plant. Use these in autumn and winter so that the plant can make use of the processed fertilizer in the spring.

Slow-release fertilizers take the form of porous granules like tiny eggs that contain small, formulated amounts of nutrients. In warmth and moisture, the pores on the granules expand, steadily releasing the fertilizer a little at a time. In cold weather, or if they are dry, the granules remain tight and the pores closed, so that the plant is not fed at inappropriate times. Slow-release fertilizer is available in different durations: three to four months; five to six months; eight to nine months. So, for example, you would pot a rooted hydrangea cutting in spring, year one, into compost mixed with a five to six-month slow-release fertilizer. This would provide nutrients for growth all summer, running out by the autumn when the young plant drops its leaves for the winter and ceases to grow. In spring, year two, it could be potted on into compost containing three to four-month granules and they would feed the plant as it grows into its pot, then continue providing nutrients for a time once it is planted out. Sometimes in a cold spring the granules do not expand and release the fertilizer: the plant might need a liquid fertilizer. Sometimes spring suddenly becomes as hot as summer. The young plants are being watered, which can result in a fast flush of growth as too much fertilizer is released from the over-expanded granules. There is little to be done except to keep the plants as cool and light as possible.

Bags of proprietary compost sometimes have the formulation of all the major nutrients and trace elements written on the side. More commonly, the bags just state whether the compost is for potting bedding plants or shrubs; whether it is for lime-hating or ericaceous plants; for water plants, orchids, and so on. But the fertilizer contained will usually have only a short life. If you are growing on shrubs, for instance, that are going to be in pots all summer long, they will grow better if you mix in some slow-release fertilizer.

Potting Up

It is tempting at the first sign of rooting to tip out the cuttings and pot them up. But it is wiser to wait until the root system is established and large enough to withstand the shock and damage of being moved.

If the cuttings have not made enough roots by the end of September it is better not to pot them up until the following February or March. Light levels between late October and early February are too low. If you were to pot up the cuttings during this period and place them somewhere frost-free, they would indeed grow in response to the warmth and the fertilizers in the compost. But they would grow tall and leggy due to the lack of light, that is, they would become etiolated. This sappy growth is very vulnerable to disease and will not make a good plant. Light suppresses growth in a plant, making plants shorter: the opposite of etiolation.

However, if the roots are growing through the drainage holes of the pot or tray by mid-September, tip the cuttings and their compost out into a larger tray to contain the excess compost. It's better not to mix that with the fresh potting compost on the potting bench.

Part-fill a small, 9cm (3½in) pot with potting compost and tip it up at an angle of 45 degrees. (A larger pot at this stage of the season could cause the cutting to continue to grow through the winter and become etiolated.) Pick up the cutting by its leaf and rest it on the compost: the roots will have plenty of room to extend to the bottom of the pot. Then fill the pot with more compost; tap it down on the bench; and make up the compost if the level is below the rim. Remove the tips of the side shoots if they are long enough.

When all the cuttings have been potted, label each with its name and pop the original label in one of the pots for reference. Then water the cuttings thoroughly with a fine rose on the watering can to settle the compost down around the roots. The final compost level should be just below the rim to allow for adequate watering and movement of air around the base of the plant.

Put the batch of cuttings in a cold frame in the autumn or near the garden tap in the summer where it's easy to keep them watered. Nip out the flower buds until the cuttings are large enough to plant out.

Pelargoniums, osteospermums and all half-hardy perennials need frost protection: a frost-free greenhouse is ideal, or a cool, light windowsill or porch should be adequate. (Check the temperature with a max:min thermometer.) Hardy deciduous shrubs and perennials would benefit from being kept in a cold greenhouse or frame over the winter. Here they will be protected from the extremes of winter wet and, providing they are put down pot-thick, that

Well-rooted cuttings of Pelargonium 'Lady Plymouth'. *The roots have visibly clung to the sides of the propagation pot.*

Separate out the cuttings. There is 100 per cent rooting success.

Pot up the cuttings.

Cold frame for hardening off cuttings.

is round pots in a honeycomb formation and square pots tight together with no gaps between the pots, their roots will be less susceptible to frost damage.

Planting Out

Half-hardy perennials will need to be kept frost-free during the winter, then hardened off in spring and brought out gradually once all danger of frost has passed. They can then be planted in their final homes.

Deciduous and evergreen shrubs will need potting on into 1ltr (5in) pots in spring, then growing on until they are big enough to be planted out either in late summer or the following spring.

Alpines will mostly need another haircut with a pair of secateurs in spring to make them bushy. But generally there is no need to pot them on from an 11cm (4½in) pot. They are mostly plants of poor soil and the haircut will prompt them into growth. They can be planted out during the summer.

Herbaceous perennials usually need the extra boost from being potted into 1ltr (5in) pots, however. They can also be planted out during the summer.

Some Hardy Geranium Cultivars

A few hardy geraniums do not make enough of a crown to allow them to be divided easily. *Geranium* 'Salome', *G.* 'Anne Thompson' and *G.* 'Ann Folkard' among others grow from one or two overwintering buds to cover an area of about 1m (3ft 3in) in all directions and flower all summer. With the first frosts, all the foliage dies back to the buds again.

As early as possible in spring, as soon as the plants start to make enough growth, take a nodal cutting in the same way as you would pelargoniums. Pot them up into 9cm (3½in) pots when they have made sufficient root growth. Then, as soon as the roots emerge from the bottom, pot them on into larger 11cm (4½in) pots, but prevent them from flowering and setting seed.

Cut back the top growth when it dies back in autumn and put the pots in a cold frame, protected from slugs and snails and where they will not get too much winter wet. They should be kept damp but not wet, or those resting buds will rot off. Plant them out the following spring when they start back into growth.

As you might imagine, these cultivars are some of the most desirable, in the over-populated genus of geraniums. As they are some of the most difficult plants to propagate, commercially they are micro-propagated.

Geranium *'Salome'*.

MICROPROPAGATION

Micropropagation is not a technique that can be taken up in the garden shed on a Sunday afternoon. It involves high-tech laboratories and white coats. But on the whole it has proved to be a useful tool in the commercial propagation of certain plants that are difficult or slow to produce, but are very sought after by the gardening public.

Briefly, a plant is selected that is true to name and as free from disease as possible. It is placed in a warm, moist, artificially lit environment and is encouraged to grow away fast. The growing tip, the meristem, is then cut from the plant and all surface contaminants are removed. This, the explant, is placed in a petrie dish on agar jelly containing a specific mix of mineral salts and sucrose. A growth hormone, cytokinin, is added to promote the formation of shoots and when the cells become a minute plant, auxins, which promote root growth, are introduced. The explant can be used repeatedly to produce innumerable new plants.

Gradually, the mini-plant grows until it is big enough to put in soil. Then the humidity is slowly reduced until the little plant is big enough to move on into small plugs. These are then totally weaned and the plugs sold on to the wholesale plant nurseries.

If it is successful, micropropagation provides a useful tool in cleaning a plant of viruses. The old double primroses, for example, were once full of virus as a result of centuries of clonal propagation (they produce no seed). Now that they have been micropropagated they are easily available and fill the garden centre shelves every spring. And because the growth hormones are still circulating strongly within their systems, they are also very much easier to divide successfully later.

It also means that if a new plant is bred it can be propagated in great numbers quickly enough to reach the gardening public in less than two years. Once it would have taken up to ten years to bulk up enough to release onto the market.

Cuttings removed.

Euphorbia characias 'Black Pearl'
*that has been cut back to produce side
shoots.*

Detach shoot with a knife.

*Prepared cuttings with cleaned heel and
lower leaves removed.*

*Cuttings inserted around the edge of the
pot.*

Cuttings watered in.

Euphorbia Characias

Many gardeners are reluctant to take cuttings from named forms and hybrids of *Euphorbia characias* in particular because of the plant's notorious milky sap. This certainly is extremely irritating to the eyes and skin, especially soft tissue. However, raising this species from seed produces especially variable plants and there are some lovely named forms and hybrids that are worthy of a little trouble. So wear disposable surgical gloves throughout the procedure and wash your hands and face well afterwards, as well as your knife and secateurs too.

Suitable cutting material usually arises from the base of the plant in spring and early summer while the plant is in flower. If not, cut back a mature shoot and it will quickly sprout suitable side shoots that can be used.

Carefully detach a young shoot, about 8–10cm (3–4in) long, from the base of the plant, either with a knife or by pulling downwards on the stem without bending it over, then detaching it. Cut off any surplus skin and remove the lower leaves just as you would any other softwood cutting. Quickly dip the cutting in hormone rooting powder to encourage the cutting to root in the normal way, then seal the cut surfaces to stop them bleeding. Remove the tip of the cutting as usual. It's at the top of the cutting, so gravity will help any bleeding to stop.

Put the cuttings around the edge of a clean pot of cuttings compost in the usual way, label and water the pot. Pop it in a plastic bag and seal it, as you would any softwood cutting, and place it under the greenhouse bench, in a shaded porch, or on a windowsill. The cuttings will root, or not, in two to three weeks and can be potted on immediately into 11cm (4½in) pots and kept somewhere cool: a cold frame is ideal. They will be ready to plant out the following spring.

Clematis

The method of taking clematis cuttings is a little different from ordinary softwood cuttings. Clematis species vary in their capacity to make root: *Clematis montana* roots quickly and easily, whereas some of the large-flowered hybrids can be very difficult indeed. In commercial situations, these difficult varieties are grafted or micropropagated.

Euphorbia × gayeri 'Betten' at the Botanic Gardens, Oxford.

Another of the problems with clematis is that they are deciduous, woody plants. They need to make enough roots to sustain their resting buds through the winter and then regenerate in spring. One of the tricks is to take the cuttings as early as possible during the growing season to allow the young plants time to grow a substantial root ball. *Clematis viticella* and *C. texensis* hybrids start making growth in early spring that can be used for cutting material as soon as it is firm enough. *Clematis montana* produces side shoots towards the end of May after flowering. The large-flowered hybrids vary. Cutting material can be taken from them as soon as suitable shoots appear on the plant.

Method

The new growth should be quite firm: neither soft and sappy, nor woody. As the cuttings will root all along the stem, not just at the nodes, the first cut should be made about 5cm (2in) below a pair of

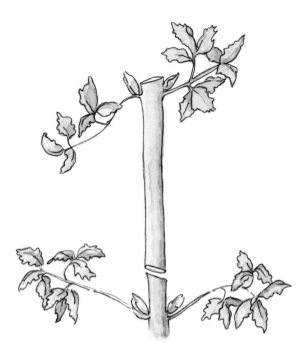

Internodal clematis cutting.

Clematis montana *'Broughton Star'*.

buds and leaflets (the node). The top cut should be just above the node. These are called internodal cuttings.

Alternatively, if the cutting material is suitable, take a cutting with two nodes. The growth buds are opposite each other in pairs at the nodes. Each node is at right angles to the previous and the next node. So burying one pair of nodes and buds gives the cutting an extra growth point. If all four buds sprout, the resulting plant will have four stems instead of two.

Collect the cutting material on a cool, damp day and place it immediately in a plastic bag while collecting to lessen the moisture loss. Clematis shoots

are very vulnerable to wilting in a very short space of time. If the weather is not perfectly cool and damp, splash a little water into the bag and always shut it tightly.

On the workbench, remove one entire leaflet and reduce the size of the opposite leaflet. Not only does this also lessen moisture loss from the cutting, but it makes them easier to handle and insert into the pot: they all point the same way without touching like banners in the breeze. If the cutting material includes two nodes, remove the lower leaves entirely.

Clematis cuttings are particularly susceptible to damping-off and rotting, so make up a fungicidal drench in a bowl or a clean bucket and dip the prepared cuttings into the mix. Allow them to drain over a piece of wire netting above a tray to collect the drips.

Fill a newly purchased pot or deep tray, with a cuttings compost mix that contains a larger proportion of washed grit to peat, or peat substitute, to increase the drainage. (A conventional seed tray will not be deep enough.) Dip the end of each dried

Young growth on Daphne tangutica.

Clematis viticella *'Prince Charles'*.

Daphne tangutica *cutting potted on in late spring.*

Daphne tangutica.

cutting into hormone rooting powder, then insert it into the pot using the end of a pencil as a dibber.

The pair of buds should just touch the surface of the compost. Make sure that the leaflets are not touching each other, the container or the bag. Label the container with the name, number of cuttings and date. Then water the cuttings by placing the pot inside a bucket until the compost is wet. Remove the pot and drain it. Watering the cuttings from overhead will simply wash off the fungicide.

Put the pot inside a big plastic bag, blow into the bag and tie up the top. Or place the tray under the plastic dome of a propagator. Place the container somewhere cool and shady: underneath the greenhouse bench is ideal, or in a cold frame.

Inspect the cuttings daily, removing any that die back. Use a fungicide powder at the first sign of a black leaf or stem and avoid overwatering them.

Aftercare

When the cuttings begin to sit up and take notice without dropping their leaves, gently take a leaflet and let it slip through your fingers. If there is a little resistance, remove the pot from the bag but leave it in the shade. (Replace the bag immediately if the cuttings droop, spray them over and try again a week later.)

When the roots appear through the holes in the bottom of the pot, tip the cuttings out carefully and pot them up into 9cm (3½in) pots. Label each little plant, while retaining the original master label in one pot. There is no need to tie them to stakes at this stage.

However, cuttings should not be potted up after the end of July. This would disturb the roots and they will not re-establish sufficiently before winter. Poorly rooted cuttings should be left in their propagation pot until the following spring.

Keep the cuttings watered so that the roots still grow, cutting back the top growth lightly after about eight weeks so as to encourage the roots to establish. The young plants should not be thinking about making flowers: any signs of motherhood should be thwarted. They need a good root system first. They should be kept in the shelter of a cold greenhouse.

In November or December, cut back all the growth to two pairs of buds and clear away the dead leaves. At this stage, the plants should be kept on the dry side until the spring. If they get too wet in winter they will succumb to fungal diseases. Take the usual precautions against mice making nests in winter and slugs fattening up in spring. All clematis cuttings will need protection at all stages of their growth from marauding slugs and snails, which can strip a batch of clematis in a night. And if the winter is mild the plants may need dusting with fungicide to prevent botrytis and stem rot.

Plants that have overwintered in their propagation pots should also have their top growth cut back. They should be potted up in spring and kept in the shelter of a frost-free greenhouse until they are hardened off in May.

Planting Out

The young clematis can then be potted into larger deep pots in May and grown on during the summer. They will need tying to a cane at this stage. Finally, they can be planted in the garden in the autumn or the following spring, when they will still need protecting from those patient slugs and snails.

Other Exceptions

Rhododendrons, azaleas and daphnes, although evergreen, can be propagated by taking softwood cuttings from about June or July with limited success. They all make new growth from behind the spent flower heads.

Cut off the spent flower head with its young growth as it becomes firm and about 5–10cm (2–4in) long. Detach each suitable shoot by grasping it between fingers and thumb and pulling downwards without bending the shoot. This will produce a flap of green skin, or a heel, which will need to be carefully trimmed off. Dip the cuttings in hormone rooting powder and continue as if they were conventional softwood cuttings. With luck, about 10 per cent of the cuttings will take, although they may not make enough roots to pot up until the following spring. They will need potting on each spring for at least two or three years before they are big enough to plant out in the garden.

PROPAGATING FROM LEAF CUTTINGS

A very few plants possess the remarkable ability to reproduce themselves from a single leaf. There are three different methods that are employed.

The first is where an entire leaf is detached from the mother plant and laid on the surface of a tray of compost. Begonia rex is the classic subject. Choose a leaf with the best typical markings and colour and, using a sharp knife, cut it off with a small length of stalk. Turn it over and make cuts about 5mm (¼in) through the thickest veins. The number will depend on the size of the leaf. Lay the leaf cut-side down, the veins underneath, on the surface of the tray of moistened basic propagation compost. Using small lengths of U-shaped wire, pin the veins down next to the cuts so that they are in close contact with the compost.

Alternatively, cut the Begonia leaf up into square sections each containing a thick piece of vein, as shown in the sequence of photographs. These are then pinned to the compost in the same way. Place the tray somewhere cool and shady and spray lightly over it regularly to keep the leaf turgid but not wet. Alternatively, cover it with the dome of a propagator. After about three or four weeks, tiny plantlets will start to form at the site of the cuts. Harden the tray off gradually and remove the plantlets carefully from the leaf and the tray. Pot them up into 9cm (3½in) pots of houseplant compost.

The second method is usually employed with *Eucomis*, *Lachenalia* and *Veltheimia*. Cut up a healthy mature leaf with a sharp knife into 4cm (1½in) sections,

Cut off leaf from Eucomis 'Zeal Bronze'.

Remove the leaf . . .

. . . and remove outer leaflet.

Slice up into sections.

Dip each section in hormone rooting powder.

Dibble in each section.

Make two rows of ten.

Tray of ten leaf cuttings.

discarding the soft tip and the base of the leaf. Insert the lower edge of each section in a tray of propagation compost and water them in well. The new plantlets will form along the baseline of the leaf. Put the tray under the dome of a propagator or somewhere shady. They should be potted up before September, when they will cease growing and die down.

The third method may be familiar to growers of African violets and *Streptocarpus* and can also be used to propagate *Peperomia*. Cut a healthy mature leaf from the mother plant with a length of leaf stalk, or petiole. The petioles are inserted upright around the rim of a pot filled with propagation compost. Water them in well, then pop the pot inside a plastic bag or under the dome of a propagator, and proceed as above.

Most plants that are propagated from leaf cuttings are house plants. They need to be actively growing when they are propagated and kept in a temperature of 16°–18°C (61°–64°F).

SEMI-RIPE CUTTINGS

Towards the autumn and early winter, the side shoots made during the summer are just starting to ripen and become more woody where they join the main stem. Cuttings of evergreen shrubs and conifers in particular are most successful if they are taken at this stage and at this time of year. Whereas deciduous shrubs are beginning to lose their leaves and become dormant for the winter, evergreens and conifers have the advantage of the retained foliage to maintain the process of photosynthesis.

However, cuttings of silver-leaved plants and evergreens that come from Mediterranean climates are usually taken during the summer (*see* Softwood Cuttings on page 40), so that they can produce plenty of roots to take them through wet winters in the UK.

When to Take Semi-Ripe Cuttings

In an average British summer, evergreens are beginning to ripen in August. However, August is full of pitfalls: heatwaves, drought and school holidays. Sometimes it's more pragmatic to wait until September. However, as with softwood cuttings, the earlier semi-ripe cuttings are taken, the more successfully they will root. Evergreen cuttings should be taken by the end of November at the latest, whereas conifer cuttings can be taken from January until the spring.

The cutting material should be just getting woody where the side shoot joins the main stem for about 1.5cm (½in). The shoot should be flexible, neither soft nor rigid, and about 10–15cm (4–6in). It's these factors that should dictate when to take the cuttings, rather than the calendar.

Method

Look for cutting material that is free from pests and diseases and is true to type. That is, make sure that any distinctive variegation is carried on the cutting material in the same way: zoned, splashed or margined. A green leaf from a variegated plant will not necessarily become variegated in the cutting.

It is particularly important with conifers to take cutting material that is growing correctly. If the plant is prostrate, that is, growing horizontally, only take cuttings of horizontal growth, not vertical shoots. The opposite is also true: take only upright cuttings of tall, thin plants, known botanically as fastigiate plants.

Junipers are a special case. They have two sorts of growth: juvenile and mature. The juvenile growth is spiky and starry, while in the mature foliage the needles lie smoother and flat to the stem. In junipers, the growth only develops from its juvenile to its mature state when the plant is grown from seed. Cuttings taken from mature growth will not make juvenile foliage. And, curiously, cuttings taken from juvenile growth will not become mature. So it is important to take cuttings with the correct foliage that is typical of the named cultivar.

From the mother plant, remove a main stem that has side shoots of about 10–15cm (4–6in) long with a sharp pair of secateurs. Collect the stems in a large plastic bag with a name label. This is especially

---

VARIEGATED PLANTS

Variegation is the appearance on the leaf of white or yellow patches or margins where the green chlorophyll is not present. This is often due to genetic factors in the make-up of the particular plant, where one type of tissue is unable to make chlorophyll and the other type of tissue is green. Because the variegation relies on the presence of these two types of tissue occurring together in the leaves, these plants must be propagated clonally from nodal cuttings. Root cuttings will not preserve this variegation, nor is it reliably transmitted by seed (although there are exceptions: aquilegias and variegated annual honesty, for example, will produce a proportion of variegated seedlings).

Because the chlorophyll is not present in part of the leaf, a variegated plant will be smaller and grow more slowly than its all-green counterpart. If a variegated plant produces an all-green shoot, it will be stronger and outgrow its variegated neighbouring shoots. This is called reversion. The shoot should be cut out completely from the mother plant before it takes over. Cuttings from such a reverted green shoot will not become variegated.

Sometimes the chlorophyll is overlaid with the red pigment, anthocyanin, which occurs in some pelargoniums, for example. Or the hairs on the leaf are a different colour from the skin, as in coloured begonias. Again, it is important to take cuttings that include all the colours in the leaves.

Sometimes there is a light blistering of air just beneath the skin, as in silver-leafed cyclamen. Blistering also occurs along the lines of the veins in *Silybum marianum* (blessed milk thistle). This variegation is more commonly passed down through seed, although the pattern of variegation will vary in the seedlings.

Hydrangea macrophylla 'Quadricolor'.

Occasionally, a virus causes a pale patterning on the surface of the leaf. Mosaic virus, for example, affects variegated abutilon, although the abutilon can withstand the infection. However, Cucumber Mosaic Virus is much more detrimental and plants have to be destroyed. (Viruses are usually specific to a particular genus, so variegated abutilons would not affect the health of cucumbers.)

A deficiency in either iron or magnesium in the plant may also cause temporary yellowing of the leaves, especially between the veins. This often occurs on an alkaline soil and an application of chelated iron or magnesium will return colour to the cheeks.

Ilex aquifolium 'Silver Queen'. *Look for suitable cutting material.*

Select a side shoot 10–15cm (4–6in) long.

Vibernum tinus. *Using a knife, pull downwards vertically . . .*

. . . detaching the shoot . . .

. . . with a heel.

Clean the excess skin from the heel.

Remove the leaves . . .

. . . against the blade of the knife.

important with different cultivars of the same genus: identifying plants from their stems and leaves is quite a skill.

Then, holding the main stem in one hand and the base of the cutting where it joins the main stem in the other hand, pull downwards vertically with the aid of a sharp knife. This should detach the cutting from the stem and include the thicker part around the junction: the basal plate. Usually there will be a length of skin, or a heel, that comes away too. Cut away the surplus skin, leaving the basal plate entire with a little tail, the heel. The basal plate contains even more phytohormones than a node, thus increasing the chances of the cutting making roots.

Heeled cutting material.

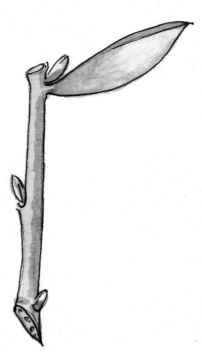

Prepared heeled cutting.

Wounding

Some evergreens are especially reluctant to make roots: hollies, garrya, rhododendrons, camellias, daphnes, Kalmia latifolia, bay laurel (*Laurus nobilis*) in particular. However, rhododendron, azalea and daphne cuttings can also be rooted from softwood material in summer (*see* Softwood Cuttings on page 40). In fact, if a plant is relatively expensive in the nursery or garden centre, it's a sure sign that it is more difficult to root from cuttings.

But there is another method of encouragement to make reluctant cuttings root: to make a wound at the bottom of the stem. This reveals more of the cambium layer beneath the skin where the roots emerge.

The basal plate is usually at an angle on the bottom of the cutting. Resting the point of the basal plate on the tip of the thumb, take an elongated, upside-down, U-shaped slice of skin off the stem at the base of the cutting. This should be on the opposite side of the cutting from the nodal bud.

A second, slighter, wound further increases the chances of rooting. Using the tip of the knife, make a single slit about 1cm (⅓in) long on the opposite side from the U-shaped wound. If the nodal bud is in the way, make the slit to one side of it. As with softwood cuttings, any lower leaves that might touch the cuttings compost should be removed with a knife from below the leaf stalk, drawing the leaf down onto the blade. Cutting the leaf off from above risks damaging the dormant bud, while pulling the leaf off can lead to skinning the cutting.

Remove the tip of the cutting. The tip is usually softer than the rest of the cutting and could draw out the moisture, or die back if it is left. But, more

To make a wound, first rest the point of the basal plate on the thumb.

Make a U-shaped wound.

Dip the prepared cutting in hormone rooting powder . . .

. . . making sure the wound is covered.

Wounded holly cutting not yet tipped out.

importantly, the tip contains all the phytohormones that make the shoot grow and suppress the growth of the lower side shoots: apical dominance.

If the cuttings have large leaves, such as bay laurel or rhododendrons, cut them in half. This reduces the amount of moisture that could be otherwise lost before the cutting has made any roots.

How Many Cuttings to Take?

Evergreens and conifers vary widely in their enthusiasm to make roots. Ultimately it's a matter of learning by experience. Especially difficult subjects are mentioned above, but hypericum, mahonia, osmanthus and pittosporum can also be tricky. It's probably worth allowing for around 50 to 70 per cent success. Pyracantha, laurel (*Prunus laurocerasus*), and viburnums are easier (70 to 80 per cent).

Conifers vary from 75 to 90 per cent success with chamaecyparis, juniperus and yew *(taxus)*, to certain species of pinus, picea, cedrus and abies, which that have such little success that they usually have to be grafted commercially.

Inserting the Cuttings

Fill a thoroughly cleaned or a new shallow pot with cuttings compost to which you could add a pinch of slow-release fertilizer (*see* page 50). Tap the container down smartly on the workbench to settle the compost just a little. Dip the end of the cutting in fresh hormone rooting powder or gel, tapping off the excess powder. There is no need to dip the cutting in water first to make the powder stick, as this just makes a glutinous ball that gums up the base of the cutting.

Insert the cuttings around the edge of the pot, making a hole with the end of a pencil or a dibber. Press the soil gently into contact with the buried stems. Make sure that the leaves are not touching the soil, the edge of the container or each other. Label each pot with the plant name, the number of cuttings and the date they were taken. In this way, you will gradually learn when and how many cuttings to take of a particular plant.

Water the cuttings in thoroughly with a fine rose on the watering can, allowing the container to drain for a few minutes. The finished soil level should be just a few millimetres below the top of the pot. Too full and water will spill over the top; too little and the gap becomes deep enough to encourage fungal growth around the necks of the cuttings.

These cuttings are mostly being taken in autumn and winter, so there is no need to cover the cuttings with a plastic bag unless the weather is unseasonably hot. Mostly it's better on balance to allow the air to circulate so as to prevent fungal disease. Put the pots somewhere shady in hot weather, but once winter is established they are better on top of the greenhouse bench or in a cold frame where you will be reminded to water them. If they flag or if the weather does becomes hot and sunny, pop the pot under the bench to let the cuttings recover.

Over the winter, some of the cuttings will die and go brown, so should be removed, while those that survive will be making roots only slowly. It is often late spring before they start to grow with any enthusiasm.

Aftercare

If, by April, the cuttings are green and happy but not actively growing, have a look to see if any roots are emerging from the bottom of the pot. It may be advantageous to give them a very dilute liquid feed at this stage if you suspect that the root system might still be small.

Sometimes an evergreen cutting looks green but refuses to grow, while its companions are all shooting away actively. When the cutting is tipped out of the compost, it will be found to have formed a thick callous at the base and no roots at all. Although making a slit across the callous with a sharp knife sometimes leads to rooting, on balance it is simpler to throw it away. Camellias and rhododendrons are particularly susceptible to this behaviour.

Once the cuttings are growing well at shoot and root, it's time to pot them up. Tip out the cuttings and their compost into a larger tray to contain the excess compost. It's better not to mix that with the fresh potting compost. Part-fill a 9cm (3½in) pot with potting compost. Rhododendrons, azaleas and camellias are lime-hating: they will need to be potted into ericaceous compost with a low pH.

Tip up the pot at an angle of 45 degrees, then pick up a cutting by its leaf and rest it on the compost. This gives plenty of room for the roots and places the cutting at the correct height in the pot. Then fill the pot with more compost and tap it down on the bench, making up the compost if the level is too low: it should be just below the rim.

When all the cuttings have been potted, label each with its name and pop the original label in one of the pots for reference. Next, water the cuttings thoroughly with a fine rose on the watering can to settle the compost down around the roots. The final compost level should be just below the rim to allow for adequate watering and movement of air around the base of the plant.

Remove the tips of the side shoots to make them grow and bush out, also taking off any flower buds. It's tempting to leave them on, but they will tend to make the plant misshapen and unbalanced. But, most importantly, they will weaken the growth of the plant.

Planting Out

Put the cuttings in a frame or somewhere shady for a few weeks to get established. If before the end of July their roots have filled the pots, move them on into larger 1ltr (5in) pots. The young plants will need to be kept in a cold frame or a cold greenhouse for the winter and moved into larger pots the following spring. Most will be large enough to be planted out that summer or autumn. Protect them from slugs and snails.

Heaths and Heathers

Heathers, that is, ericas and callunas, are successfully taken as semi-ripe cuttings between June and August. Strip them of their needles by running them between your forefinger and thumb, then pinch out the growing tip. This leaves a cutting about 2cm (¾in) long. Arrange them either in a grid pattern in a seed tray, or individually into small plug trays. They are usually 80 to 90 per cent successful.

PH

The term pH is shorthand for indicating the levels of acidity and alkalinity in the soil. These levels are given in a scale from 0–14, where 7 is theoretically neutral (although a pH of 6.5 is effectively neutral for plants). The lower the number, the more acidic the soil; the higher the number, the more alkaline. It is a logarithmic scale, that is, each change of number is an increase or decrease by a factor of ten. So, for example, pH5 is ten times more acidic than pH6, while pH5 is 100 times more acidic than pH7.

Some plants are specifically adapted to grow in acid soil: rhododendrons, camellias, heathers, to name but a few. On the other hand, carnations, chrysanthemums and daffodils, for example, grow better in limey soils with a high pH. High levels of acidity or alkalinity cause some of the nutrients to be only partially available to plants and certain plants are unable to take up and use those nutrients. Kits are available from the garden centre to test your garden soil. Alternatively, take a look at what is growing healthily in your neighbours' gardens. Are there lots of rhododendrons? If so, your soil is probably acidic.

Whereas it is quite easy to neutralize a very acidic soil with a dressing of lime, it is much more difficult to make a limey soil neutral or acidic without destroying the life of the soil. Flowers of Sulphur can be added to neutralize alkaline soil, but it is wiser to work with the existing pH levels in the soil and grow ericaceous, acid-loving plants only in containers.

The texture of the soil, whether it is sandy or heavy clay, has no bearing on the pH. But if you do have acid clay, the soil can be lightened a little by dressing it with lime. This will neutralize the acidity, however, and you will be unable to grow rhododendrons and camellias well.

Sarcococca confusa *(Christmas Box) in year two. It will be ready to plant out in year three.*

Cornus alba *(dogwood).*

Although heather cuttings are taken in the summer, they should be left in their propagation trays until the following spring. Standing them on a bed of sharp sand will encourage root growth, which in turn promotes plenty of healthy top growth.

By March or April, they will be eager to be moved on. Pick up the propagation tray from the sand bed, pulling the roots out gently from the sand. Then with an old bread knife slice off all the layer of hairy roots that has emerged through the drainage holes. This rough-and-ready root pruning causes the plants to make more fresh roots and grow away faster. Callunas should then be potted up into an ericaceous mix, while ericas are more tolerant of a neutral potting compost.

Loosely fill a 9cm (3½in) pot with the correct compost, plunge your index finger into the middle and insert the cutting into the hole. Tap the pot down on the bench and fill it up if necessary. When all the heathers have been potted up, take a pair of sharp secateurs and give them all a haircut to make them bushy and to equalize the shoots at the top with the roots at the bottom.

HARDWOOD CUTTINGS

By the end of the year, the current season's growth on deciduous shrubs has hardened up and become woody. The leaves have dropped off and all the sugars have been turned into starches and stored

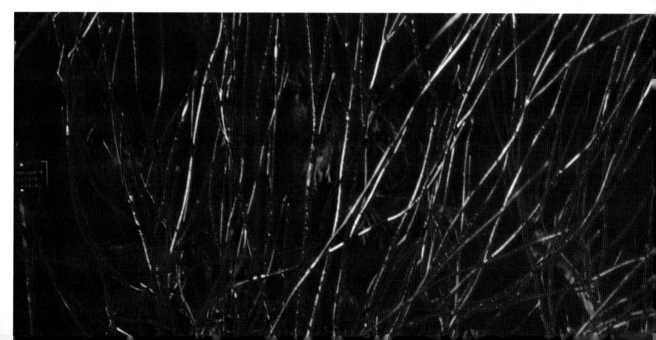

in the stems. This is the ideal time to take hardwood cuttings of deciduous shrubs that would root easily at any time, but this method takes advantage of a quiet time in the garden.

However, not all deciduous shrubs root that easily. Any flower arranger will know that some plant stems will make roots if they are left in a jug of water too long: pussy willows (*salix*), for example. Unfortunately, these roots are especially adapted to growing in water and the stems need to make new soil-growing roots. Luckily they are in rooting mode so this is also easily achieved.

Some climbing plants, such as ivy (*Hedera*) or *Hydrangea petiolaris*, cling to their hosts with adapted roots. These roots are unable to grow and feed in the soil and where the plant touches the ground new roots develop to enable the plant to grow. Plants that have adapted roots are probably easier than most to strike from cuttings, but it is still quicker and more successful to root them in the conventional way.

Hydrangea petiolaris *climbing a tree.*

Hardwood cuttings are also very successful with dogwoods (*Cornus alba*), blackcurrants, red and white currants, ornamental currants (*Ribes*), poplars, elder (*Sambucus nigra*) and snowberries. But forsythia, winter jasmine, kerria, privet, honeysuckles, perovskia and caryopteris are also worth trying.

When to Take Hardwood Cuttings

The most successful times are soon after the plant has dropped its leaves in late autumn, or just before the buds begin to swell in early spring. But as these plants root easily, any time during the winter is usually successful.

Method

Sharp, scissor-cut secateurs can be used throughout the process of taking these hard, woody cuttings. There is no need to wield a knife. Take a long piece (30cm/12in) of the current year's growth that has ripened sufficiently for the stem to become woody and rigid. It should ideally be pencil thick where appropriate. Fatter cuttings make buxom plants. So on naturally thinner-stemmed subjects like kerria, honeysuckles, perovskia and caryopteris, choose the thickest of the current year's wood with good stores of starch.

Ensure that the cutting is undamaged, that is, the skin is intact and unblemished and is true to type. Variegated plants will have dropped their leaves, so you need to have removed any reverted green growth during the growing season.

Cut off the top few buds just above a leaf node. They will probably not be fully ripe. Then make another clean cut with secateurs just beneath a lower node. The final length of the cutting can vary from 15cm (6in) to 30cm (12in), according to the plant material available.

Inserting the Cuttings

There are then two methods of inserting the prepared cuttings: they can either be inserted in a trench in the open ground; or put in pots in a cold greenhouse or frame.

The first method is suitable for plants that root particularly easily: willows, dogwoods, currants,

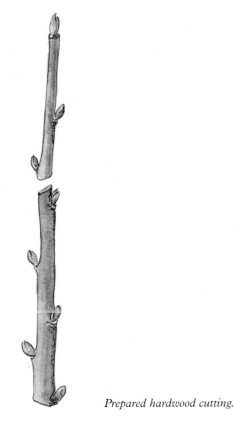

Prepared hardwood cutting.

bottom or the sides of the pot. If the cuttings are a little flexible, use the end of a pencil as a dibber to insert them so as to avoid bending their stems. These cuttings should also be two-thirds buried. Label the pot with the name, date and number of cuttings and water it thoroughly. Finally, put the pot in a cold greenhouse or frame for the winter.

During the winter, inspect the cuttings regularly and remove any that go brown before they infect their neighbours. Keep them watered, especially in sunny weather: the compost has very sharp drainage.

Aftercare

In March, remove any cuttings from the trench that have not rooted. Those that remain and are beginning to show signs of life should be pruned back to two or three buds from the ground to make them bush out. They can be lifted at any time from the autumn and replanted into their final positions.

As soon as the cuttings in the pots show signs of life in spring, tip them out onto a tray on the potting bench. They can be either potted up into 2ltr (6in) pots, or planted out in a spare piece of ground to grow on. They should have good root systems. Any cuttings that have only a few roots can be put together in a pot or the ground. Two weaklings together can give the appearance of one strong plant. Prune them down to two or three buds to make them bush out. They will be ready to plant out either in the autumn or the following spring according to their size.

poplars, elder and snowberries, for example. Choose a sunny, sheltered spot in the garden that is clear of weeds and where the soil is fertile but drains well. Even these cuttings will be reluctant to root into cold, wet, heavy soil. Insert a spade to its full depth and lean it back to open a V-shaped trench but with one vertical side. Put a layer of horticultural grit along the bottom to improve the drainage. Then insert the cuttings so that they will be two-thirds below the soil level, leaning against the vertical side of the trench. Refill the trench with soil, label the row with the name, date and number of cuttings, then water them in.

The second method is for slightly trickier plants, such as forsythia, jasmine, kerria and so on. Make up a very gritty cuttings mix, the higher the proportion of grit included the better, then very loosely fill a 2ltr (6in) deep pot with the mix. (Shorter cuttings can have shorter pots.) Next, push the base of the prepared cuttings into the compost all around the edge of the pot without letting them touch the

LAYERING

The propagation of shrubs by layering, that is rooting shoots while they are still attached to the mother plant, is a very easy way to root more difficult shrubs. It can be used on *Cornus controversa*, witch hazel, magnolia, parrotia, rhododendron and azaleas, for example, but this list is by no means exhaustive. It's a method that could be used on any shrub whose lowest shoots will reach the ground.

Although most subjects will take a year to root (magnolias, rhododendrons and azaleas take eighteen months), the end result, a garden-ready plant, is achieved more quickly than by taking cuttings.

Magnolia × soulangeana.

The only disadvantage might be that only one or two plants can be produced in this way at any one time.

When to Layer

Ideally, layering should be carried out between March and June. The shrubs are growing actively and quickly and the ground is warm.

Method

Take a strong young shoot that was produced the previous year. It's going to be pegged down to the ground, so your choice of propagating material will be quite limited in many cases.

But before pegging the shoot down, it must be wounded to interrupt the flow of sap and encourage the roots to form. There are two methods of wounding. The first, and the simplest, is to twist the shoot sharply so that the stem tissue is damaged about 30cm (12in) from the tip. The second is more formal. With a sharp knife, make a cut halfway through the lower side of the stem nearest the ground, about 30cm (12in) from the tip. When the tip is bent up, the cut will open and the wood will form a tongue.

This cut remains open when the shoot is pegged down.

Push the stem down at the wounded point so that it makes contact with the soil and pin it with wire hoops to anchor it. The hoops can easily be made with galvanized wire cut up into 15cm (6in) lengths and bent over like a hairpin.

Then bend the tip of the shoot up from the point of contact with the ground and tie it in an upright position to a cane. This keeps the cut wound open;

Select a shoot of the previous year's growth. Cut halfway through the stem, then peg it down, opening up the wound.

ensures that the finished plant is growing upright and not at an angle; and helps to anchor it in position.

Cover the wound with 10cm (4in) of soil to prevent the layer from drying out. A flat stone placed on top also helps to keep the wound in close contact with the soil and retain the moisture. Other layers taken from the same plant should be kept at least 15cm (6in) apart to prevent any root competition.

Aftercare

The layers will need watering in dry weather and kept weed-free throughout the summer. With the exceptions mentioned above, most plants will have made sufficient roots by the following spring to allow them to be separated from their parents.

Potting Up or Planting Out

The following spring, when the layer has made plenty of roots, carefully remove the soil covering the umbilical stem from the mother plant to the layer. Remove the cane and the pin. Then gently lift the layer from the ground with a fork so that you can see where to cut the stem.

Cut the umbilical stem as closely as possible to the rooted part of the shoot without damaging the roots. If a large snag is left it can rot and cause disease in the young plant. Then cut the remaining part of the umbilical stem as closely as you can to the mother plant, for the same reason. Remove the

Lift the layered shoot.

growing tip of the new plant to make it bush up and do not allow it to make flower in this, its first year. That way, the plant will make a better root system.

Ideally, the young plants should be potted up into 2ltr (6in) pots: they have taken a year to root and deserve the best treatment you can give them. They are also shrubs that would be expensive to replace in terms of time and money.

Keep the pots somewhere shaded and water them throughout the summer. They will be ready to plant out that autumn or the following spring, depending on their size. Alternatively, they can be grown on in a spare area of ground until they are big enough to join their companions in the garden. But ensure that the soil is in good heart, free from weeds and with lots of organic matter dug in beforehand. Keep the plants well watered in dry weather.

However, there are some variations to this classic method.

Ferns

The majority of ferns have to be propagated either by division in late winter or by sowing their spores, but some species of the genus *Polystichum* and × *woodwardias* have a trick up their leaves. They make plantlets all along their leaves in the autumn, which can be layered and rooted very easily.

By late autumn, a careful look at the fronds of polystichum will reveal little knots of fresh green growth at the junction of the leaflets with the main leaf stem. Bend the entire frond down so that it makes close contact with the soil and pin it down with wire 'hairpins' along its length. Cover the stem with a little peat or peat substitute so that the green plantlets are still showing. Leave it through the winter, just checking occasionally to make sure that the layers have not been lifted by the frost or heavy rain.

Alternatively, the leaf can be cut off and pinned down in a seed tray filled with cuttings compost. Again, cover the stem lightly with a little compost or horticultural grit, label the tray with the name and date and water it. The tray can be placed under the bench in a cold greenhouse or in a frame.

By the following spring, the little fernlets will have rooted, or not. They are then cut into individual

Leaf of Polystichum setiferum *'Divisilobum'* pinned down to the soil.

Polystichum setiferum *'Divisilobum'* in winter with plantlets along the central ribs of the leaves.

A fern leaf cut off and placed on a tray of compost.

Insert the pins to hold the leaf in contact with the compost.

The leaf pinned down.

Young fern potted up and growing on; it will be ready for planting out next spring.

Aster thomsonii *'Nanus'*.

plants and potted up into 9cm (3½in) pots of ordinary potting compost. They will be ready for planting out the following spring.

Heathers

Although heather *(erica* or *calluna)* cuttings are quite easy to take as cuttings (see Semi-Ripe Cuttings on page 59), they are even easier to root by a modified form of layering. This is especially useful with old, woody plants that need to be replaced.

In the autumn, cover the heather with peat or peat substitute so that only the tips of the shoots are showing. Mound it up and work the peat/peat substitute into the plant with your hands. Water the mound heavily into the crown to settle the peat in thoroughly. You may find the peat needs topping up as the winter rains wash it away.

By spring, the little shoots should have rooted. Excavate them very carefully with a hand fork, or, better still, your fingers. Alternatively, if the mother plant is overdue a visit to the compost heap, lift the entire plant with a fork, give it a gentle shake and put it in a tray on the potting bench. Detach each rooted shoot from the crown of the plant, then pot it up into ericaceous compost in a 9cm (3½in) pot. If you have too many rooted shoots, put three to a pot to make a bushier plant faster. When they are all potted up, give them a haircut, removing the growing tips, with a pair of sharp secateurs. Finally, label the little plants and water them in.

Keep the new plants well irrigated during the summer; they should be ready to plant out by the autumn. *Callunas* need an acid soil, but many of the *ericas*, the winter-flowering heathers, are more tolerant of alkaline conditions.

BASAL CUTTINGS

Some herbaceous plants form a crown that is far too tight to be able to split easily without doing serious damage: for example, named delphinium cultivars, dahlias, lupins, chrysanthemums, Michelmas daisies (*Aster*), *Helenium* 'Moerheim Beauty', *Campanula lactiflora* 'Loddon Anna', *Thalictrum* 'Hewitt's Double'. Alternatively, it may be impractical or undesirable to lift the crown of a particular plant, even though more may be wanted elsewhere in the garden. The answer is to take cuttings from the base of the plant without disturbing the whole plant, that is, basal cuttings.

When to Take Basal Cuttings

There is only a brief opportunity to take cuttings when growth starts from the crown in spring. Wait until the shoots have pushed up from the crown to a height of about 10–15cm (4–6in). Any later and many stems will have become too tall, woody, or, in the case of delphiniums, hollow.

Method

Using an old knife, run the blade down the shoot into the soil and detach it as low down as possible.

Basal growth arising too tightly to the previous years' growth, thereby preventing the plant being divided.

Sometimes the shoots will have made small roots.

The resulting cutting should be white at the base where it has been underground. Sometimes it will already have one or two small roots.

Remove any lower leaves that might come in contact with the compost by cutting them against the blade held beneath the leaf. There is a dormant bud in the axil, the junction, between the leaf and the stem. Cutting down from above could damage that bud, while pulling the leaves off with finger and thumb could result in stripping the skin off below the axil.

Remove the tip of the cutting if it is possible. Very often, this part is 'soft'. It droops very quickly and is vulnerable to fungal disease. More importantly, the tip is full of hormones that will either produce flowers, rather than roots, or make the shoot grow upwards rather than branch out sideways at the leaf axils: apical dominance. By removing the tip full of the 'wrong' hormones, the resulting plant will start in the right frame of mind: producing roots rather than flowers and making a bushy shaped plant rather than a beanstalk. If the tip is not visible, remove it as soon as growth makes it possible.

Unless the weather is very cool and damp, cut the leaves by a third to reduce the loss of moisture from the leaves' surfaces. The cutting cannot replace any moisture lost without a root system.

When deciding how many cuttings to take, prudence dictates that it is always wise to allow for a minimum of 10 per cent loss from cutting to mature plant. Basal cuttings are usually at least 90 per cent successful.

Run the blade down the shoot into the soil.

Basal cuttings.

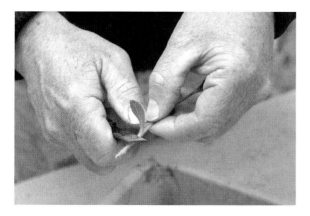

Remove the lower leaves . . .

. . . and tip it out.

Inserting the Cuttings

Loosely fill to the brim a clean or new shallow pot with cuttings compost. A seed tray is not usually deep enough. Tap the pot smartly down on the workbench to settle the compost a little.

Seal the end of each cutting by contacting just the very tip with a little fungicide powder, or hormone rooting powder that contains fungicide. This will stop any rot getting into the cutting through the open wound.

Then position the cuttings around the edge of the pot using the end of a pencil to make a planting hole. Press the soil gently into contact with the buried stems. The leaves should not touch each other, the soil or the edge of the pot.

Water the pot thoroughly with a fine rose on the watering can and leave it to drain for a few minutes.

The finished soil level should be just a few millimetres below the top of the pot. Too full and water will spill over the top; too little and the gap becomes deep enough to encourage fungal growth around the necks of the cuttings. Label each pot with the plant name, the number of cuttings and the date they were taken. In this way, you will gradually learn when and how many cuttings to take of a particular plant.

Put the pot inside a big plastic bag. Blow into the bag with your breath, which is rich in CO_2. Plants inhale CO_2 and exhale oxygen. This will also keep the sides of the bag from touching the cutting. Then tie up the top of the bag tightly with twisty wire ties. Place the finished pot somewhere cool and shady. Under the bench in the greenhouse is ideal, or on a cool windowsill, or in a shady porch.

Dip the cutting in hormone rooting powder.

Dibble in the cutting.

Firm in the cuttings . . .

. . . around the edge of the pot . . .

Open the plastic bag every day or two to allow the condensation to drip down to the bottom of the bag and remove any cuttings that have gone brown. They would otherwise be a source of infection. Blow into the bag again, retie it and put the pot back.

The cuttings should have rooted, or not, in about two weeks. They will look perkier: the buds of the side shoots will just be starting to swell and a very gentle feel of the leaf tip will meet with just a little resistance. Obviously it is important not to tug on the leaves and break any tiny hair-like roots beneath.

Aftercare

Once you are sure the cuttings have started to root, leave the plastic bag open for a couple of days, then remove the pot from the bag altogether. If the cuttings look dry, water them a little, but resist the temptation to flood them: their roots are minimally active and the cutting could still rot off.

Once you are confident the cuttings are rooted and growing, remove the pot to the top of the green-house bench or a sunnier windowsill. If the cuttings flag and go limp again, spray them over with fresh water and put the pot back into a shadier position.

Potting Up

When the cuttings are clearly growing actively and the roots are through the drainage holes in the pot, tip out the whole contents carefully into an empty seed tray. This contains the excess cuttings compost

. . . and water them in.

within the seed tray, as well as being easier to handle the young plants.

Holding each plant carefully in your hand, place it in a small pot half-filled with potting compost, tipped at an angle of 45 degrees. This gives plenty of room for the roots and places the cutting at the correct height in the pot. Then, holding the cutting gently, straighten up the pot again and fill it to the brim with more compost. Tap the pot down firmly on the workbench and top it up with compost if necessary. Label each plant clearly, keeping the original label (the master label) in the batch for reference.

Once all the cuttings have been potted up and labelled give them a good watering and put them somewhere shady and out of the weather: a cold frame is ideal. In this way you can ensure that they don't get exhausted in the sun, or flooded in a storm. And keep them watered.

If you were unable to remove the tip of the cutting at the outset, using a sharp pair of secateurs, cut it off as it extends. This will make it bush out. With basal cuttings, however, this need only be done once at the outset.

Planting Out

Basal cuttings should be ready for planting out by mid to late summer depending on their size and potential location. Alternatively, pot them on before the end of July and keep them in a cold frame over

---

DAHLIA CUTTINGS

Dahlias are easy to propagate from cuttings taken as the young shoots emerge from the dormant tubers in spring. They will flower later than those produced on the main tuber, so that if you put them next to the mother tubers the flowering season will extend into the autumn.

Lift the tubers after the first frosts of autumn have blackened the foliage. Cut the stems back to 15cm (6in) and lift the tubers with a fork, taking care not to damage them. If any damage does occur cut that part away with a clean knife and dust the cut with a fungicidal powder such as green sulphur. Place the tubers upside down for a week, stems to the floor, to allow the moisture to drain away. Then pack them in a single layer in a deep tray with peat or vermiculite around the tubers. Keep the point where the stems join the tubers, the crown, above the level of peat or vermiculite. Dust the crowns with more green sulphur powder to prevent rotting and keep the peat or vermiculite just on the damp side of bone dry under the bench in a frost-free greenhouse, shed or garage.

During the winter check the tubers from time to time to make sure that they have not gone mouldy or shrivelled. If any are mouldy, discard them, empty the tray and start again with healthy tubers and fresh peat or vermiculite, plus a dusting of green sulphur powder. If they are shrivelled, soak them overnight in a bucket of water in the garage or shed, not outdoors, and return them to the tray.

In spring, bring the tubers out into the light of a frost-free greenhouse and water them lightly and regularly. They will soon start to produce fleshy green shoots from the top of the tubers. Leaving one or two intact to grow the tuber on, other shoots can be removed with a sharp knife as near the junction with the tuber as possible. They should be about 7–10cm (2¾–4in) long. Choose the thickest shoots with short gaps between the side buds (the internodes). Remove the tip and the lower pair of leaves and tidy up the cut if it's necessary. Dip the bottom of the shoot dry in hormone rooting powder and tap off the excess. Fill a small 7cm (2¾in) pot with propagation compost, tap it down and, using a pencil,

Dahlia *'Bishop of Llandaff'*.

dibble a hole. Insert the shoot to a depth of about 2cm (¾in) and gently firm it with your fingers. Water it in to settle the compost, label it with the name and date, then put it under the dome of a propagator or in a plastic bag. Blow into the bag and tie up the top. Put the pots in a frost-free greenhouse,, or on a shady windowsill. A faster alternative would be to use a covered electric propagator or a heated bench under a plastic tent. The thermostat should be set at 10°C (50°F).

When the cuttings start to push out side shoots, harden them off gradually by opening the bag or propagator, or cooling down the bench. Then when the roots start to appear through the bottom of the pots, move them on into 1ltr (5in) pots of general compost. Pinch out the growing tips again to make the plant produce more growing points that will eventually flower.

Harden off the pots when all danger of frost has passed by moving them in and out of the greenhouse day and night, for about a week. They will then be ready to plant out or pot on again. They should flower by late July or early August, depending on the weather.

the winter. Plant them out in spring and they will flower that year.

ROOT CUTTINGS

It may be surprising to learn that some plants can regenerate from their roots without any top growth attached. Until, that is, you remember the last occasion you tried to move an oriental poppy (*Papaver orientale*), an acanthus or a Japanese anemone (*Anemone* × *hybrida*). It was carefully dug up and transported to its new home, where it thrived, and the space it left was replanted with something different. Then, after a few months, little sprouts of poppy, acanthus or anemone started to appear in and around the newcomer, and very soon the incumbent was back: still in residence. It had regenerated from the tiny bits of root left in the soil.

But it's not just the obvious candidates that can grow from root cuttings: *Primula denticulata*, named verbascum, and *Eryngium bourgatii* cultivars, for example, can all perform this trick. Some gardening encyclopaedias give this information, but mostly

Papaver orientale *'Effendi'.*

other keen propagators are happy to share their experiences. On page 79 is a list of plants known to grow from root cuttings, but it is not comprehensive. Add to it when you can.

But why go to all the trouble of taking root cuttings? Clearly it is a useful method if you simply want more of a particular plant without disturbing the original: it's too small to divide, for instance; or it's growing in an awkward place and is not thriving; or, as in the case of verbascums, it might kill the original plant to dig it up entirely. But it's also a reliable method of making a quantity of one particular cultivar.

When to Take Root Cuttings

The best time is undoubtedly towards the end of the winter, in January or February, while the plant is still dormant, but before spring kicks it into active growth. Too early and the pieces of root can rot away. They tend to get watered by default in the greenhouse while they are not growing and making use of that water. Too late and the shoots are already growing: brittle and easily damaged.

Oriental poppies are a little unusual in that their dormant season is in the late summer. They make rosettes of leaves during the autumn and then stand still for the winter. As plants of well-drained soil, they are very vulnerable to rotting, however, so the most successful time to take root cuttings is at the same time as the others, in late winter.

Method

If you can dig up the dormant plant it is clearly easier to get to the roots. But, if digging up is not a good option, take a small hand fork and carefully excavate around one side of the dormant crown. When you have located a good fat root, about a pencil thickness, use an old but sharp knife to detach it from the crown as far up as possible. Try not to leave any of the mother plant's top growth high and dry without any roots attached. The idea is to leave it undisturbed, not marooned. Settle the soil back in around the mother plant and give it a drink.

Cut up the root into sections 2–5cm (¾–2in) long, making a horizontal cut at the top of the cutting where it was nearest the crown and a sloping

LIST OF PLANTS THAT CAN BE PROPAGATED FROM ROOT CUTTINGS

This is not a comprehensive list of plants that will regenerate from root cuttings. Some are easier than others; some are easier from division if you only need a few more plants. All the species of the following genera can be propagated from root cuttings unless stated otherwise:

- *Acanthus*
- *Anchusa*
- *Anemone japonica (A. hybridus)*
- *Arabis*
- *Asclepias*
- *Campsis radicans*
- *Chaenomeles*
- *Cirsium rivulare 'Atropurpureum'*
- *Crambe cordifolia*
- *Dicentra spectabilis*
- *Dicentra spectabilis 'Alba'*
- *Echinops ritro*
- *Eryngium*
- *Incarvillea*
- *Morisia monantha*
- *Papaver orientale*
- *Paulownia tomentosa*
- *Phlox paniculata*
- *Primula denticulata* (but not other *Primula* species)
- *Prunus padus*
- *Pulmonaria* (some but not all species)
- *Pulsatilla vulgaris*
- *Rhus typhina* (also *R. copallina, R. glabra*)
- *Robinia*
- *Romneya coulteri*
- *Rubus spectabilis* (and some other *Rubus* species)
- *Sambucus*
- *Saponaria ocymoides*
- *Statice*
- *Stokesia laevis*
- *Symphytum*
- *Trollius*
- *Verbascum*

a)

b)

*a) The semi-dormant root of an Oriental poppy (*Papaver orientale*).*

b) The cut-up root, with a horizontal cut at the top and a sloping cut at the base.

a)

b)

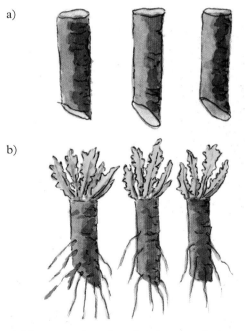

a) The root cuttings cleaned and ready to be inserted vertically in the compost.

b) The root cuttings produce their own roots and shoots.

cut at the base, so that if the cat comes along and knocks them all onto the floor you will know which way up they should be. The 'polarity' matters: only the top will produce shoots; only the bottom will extend down into root growth.

Do not use hormone rooting powder: it's the shoots that are missing, not the roots. But it can help to put the prepared cuttings in a plastic bag

Anemone hybrida *'Honorine Jobert'*.

Shoots arising from the roots of a Japanese anemone.

containing a little fungicide powder and shake them about. This will help to prevent them rotting.

Japanese anemones are a little different. They produce little white nodules on their roots. These are tiny buds, about 2mm (⅛in) in height, which quickly become white underground shoots. Cut 2–3cm (¾–1⅛in) sections of root containing at least one bud. These should be placed horizontally as described below. Pull the tail end of the cut root out from the ground if you can, so that it does not cause rot in the mother plant's root ball, and discard it.

How Many Cuttings to Take?

If there are plenty of roots available for cuttings, allow for a 10 to 20 per cent loss. However, mostly the number of cuttings taken is limited by the size of the root system of the plant. Meanness does not pay off: if you take smaller sections of root, then the resulting plants will also be smaller and they will take an extra year to grow big enough to plant out.

Inserting the Cuttings

Take a deep pot (a cleaned-out old chrysanthemum pot is ideal) and fill it loosely to the brim with cuttings compost, tapping the pot down on the workbench to settle the compost down. Then, using a dibber or an old pencil, insert the root cuttings vertically around the edge of the pot, ensuring they are the right way up. The cut surface at the top of each cutting should be on a level with the surface of the compost. Water the cuttings in with a fine rose on the watering can. The tops of the cuttings will end up a little proud of the compost surface. Cover the cuttings and the compost with a layer of coarse horticultural grit. Label them with plant name, number of cuttings taken and the date. Finally, put the pots somewhere cool and shady like a cold frame or under the greenhouse bench.

Some plants such as eryngium, Japanese anemones and *Primula denticulata* produce roots that are too thin and bendy to insert vertically. These cuttings can be laid out horizontally on the surface of a seed tray filled with cuttings mix compost. They grow more untidily than vertically produced cuttings, so it is important to leave plenty of space around each cutting for easier handling later. Alternatively, they can be put individually into plug trays, which makes them easier to handle when potting up.

Oriental poppies are particularly brittle and for this reason plug trays are often used for these root cuttings (*see* the section on Tools and Equipment in Part 3). Choose a tray with extra large plugs, or holes, to contain the root system. It can be confusing to mix different Oriental poppy cultivars within one tray, so choose smaller trays with the optimum number of holes that take up less space and keep the poppy cultivars separate: each cultivar in its own tray.

Place the pots or plug trays on top of the greenhouse bench or in a cold frame and keep them lightly watered. They need light rather than heat. If they are placed in a heated propagator or on the relative warmth of a spare-room windowsill, the roots will become exhausted, shrivel up and fail to shoot.

Aftercare

Within a few weeks, green leaves will appear through the gravel. It is very tempting to think that they are ready for potting, but mostly they are not. The top growth comes first, followed by the root growth.

Potting Up

Wait until the roots are visible through the drainage holes at the bottom of the pot or plug tray before you tip them out. This is the most precarious stage of the enterprise. The root system is heavy with gritty cuttings compost and the shoots are fragile. For this reason it is important to handle the plantlets like baby birds and not pick them up by their leaves as you would a seedling: the heavy root ball detaches itself from the shoots and all is lost.

Plugs will simply pop out by pushing them up from the bottom with the end of a pencil. Or it is possible to buy a special spiky board that matches the trays exactly. Place the plug-tray on top of the board and push down gently, and all the plugs will bounce out eagerly.

Pot up the plantlets into 9cm (3½ins) pots, water them, and label each one. Keep the original label (the master label) in the batch for reference. Put the pots in a cold greenhouse, a cold frame or a very cool porch or conservatory, for a few weeks until the worst of the winter is past. They are frost hardy, but need slowly 'hardening off' or weaning away from their nursery conditions and acclimatizing to conditions outside. Then in April or May, when spring is in sight, move them to a sheltered spot outside for the summer where you can keep an eye on them. And keep them watered.

Some of the larger, more vigorous plants such as acanthus, Japanese anemones, oriental poppies and verbascums will probably need potting on into larger 1tr (5in) pots by June or July. But after the end of July it is better to leave them in their existing containers for the winter. They should be ready for planting out in the garden once they have made plenty of top growth in the following spring.

RHIZOMES

Rhizomes are swollen stems that lie on top of the soil and root down into it. The leaves and flowers usually arise at the end of the rhizome, but all along its length are dormant buds in what appear to be creases. They are adapted axils. Bearded iris, bergenias and epimedium are easy to propagate in this way, but each plant has its own method and timing.

When to Divide Rhizomes

Bearded iris and epimediums are ideally cut up and divided after flowering, but before July. They then have the remainder of the summer in which to get their new roots down into the warm soil before they go dormant for the winter. Other herbaceous irises, such as *Iris sibirica* or *I. ensata*, should be split after flowering. The bulbous irises such as late winter flowering rockery irises (*I. reticulata*) produce offsets that can be grown on for a few years until they are big enough to flower. It is mainly the bearded irises that produce rhizomes.

Bergenias are best lifted and cut up during the winter: January and February. The resulting plants are potted up in the spring and have an entire season to grow into sizeable plants.

Method: Bearded Irises

The crowns of bearded iris often get very congested. Weeds become entrenched between the tightly packed rhizomes and the centre of the plant dies off. So it is no disadvantage to the plant to lift it after flowering and extricate the weeds in order to split it.

Bearded irises.

Examine the lifted and cleaned crown of the rhizomes. Cut down the flowered stems and reduce the fans of leaves by half, cutting them at an angle. This helps to reduce the loss of moisture while the roots get going again. Remove any leaves that show signs of spotting, as this is an endemic fungal disease of iris. Spray them with a fungicide.

Cut out radically and discard any rhizomes that have gone soft and rotted, dusting the cut ends of the remaining rhizomes with fungicidal powder. Then, with a sharp but old knife, cut up the crown into sections, also discarding the old rhizomes in the middle of the plant. Each division should have one or two portions of rhizome with roots attached and a fan of leaves. The dormant buds will be almost invisibly tucked in the axils of the rhizomes.

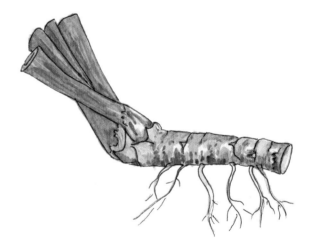

Division of a bearded iris rhizome.

Aftercare: Bearded Irises

The divided irises can be replanted straight away, after improving the soil with organic matter. On very heavy soils, bearded irises can be difficult to establish. The addition of coarse grit into the planting hole will help the drainage. Plant the rhizomes so that they sit on the surface of the ground, preferably facing south. The fan of leaves will be on the opposite, north side of the plant. There needs to be plenty of sun on those rhizomes to make them flower well. Water them in, remembering to keep them watered if the weather turns hot and dry.

Method: Epimediums

Epimediums make wonderful ground cover in a shady garden and are easy to propagate after flowering. They can, of course, simply be lifted with a

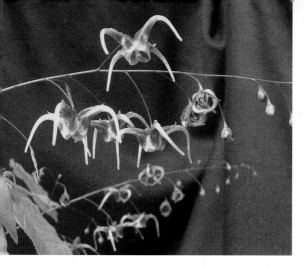
Epimedium × omeiense 'Emei Shan'.

garden fork and the crowns teased apart with the aid of a few strategic cuts of their thin rhizomes, but to make several more of them it is better to be a bit more painstaking.

Knock off as much soil as possible from the lifted crown so that you can see where to make a cut. Epimediums grow in little clumps that attach to each other with rhizomes, so cut the connecting rhizomes to make generous clumps with plenty of root attached. Don't be mean. If they are too small, they will surrender to the forces of fungal disease before their roots can get going.

Aftercare: Epimediums

The clumps can be replanted into improved ground, or potted up and kept until next spring in a cold frame, then planted out. It is a question of whether their new home has bossy neighbours that will take them over, or if it has lots of room for them to settle down. Either way, the watering regime should be the same: settle them in with a good soak and keep them watered in hot, dry spells.

Method: Bergenias

The rhizomes of bergenias can simply be lifted, cut up into large sections and replanted, discarding the oldest part of the plant, or they can be propagated in a similar way to root cuttings (*see* page 78). During the winter, lift a section of the mother plant and wash off the soil thoroughly. Bergenias are parti-

cularly susceptible to the attentions of vine weevils. These little pests lay their microscopic eggs around the rhizome. When they hatch, the greedy larvae burrow into their bed-and-breakfast rhizome and hollow it out completely.

Cut off the leaves at the end of the rhizome, then cut it into pieces 2½–5cm (1–2in) long. Each section should have a dormant bud just visible in the axil of the rhizome. Dust the cut ends of the sections with fungicidal powder to prevent them rotting. And place them in rows, without touching, on a seed tray filled with cuttings compost. They need not be buried. Just press them down into the compost leaving the dormant buds showing on top.

If they seem a little loose and wayward on the surface of the compost, dress the tray with a layer of coarse horticultural grit to anchor the pieces. If they don't make contact with the compost they will not root. Water the tray, label it with the name, number of cuttings and date, and put it on the bench in a cold greenhouse or a frame.

Bergenias can also be propagated in late July and early August. Take the end growth of each rhizome and remove the base of the old leaves very carefully. New roots can be seen pushing through the stem. Then treat them as before. The plants will be ready to plant out the following spring.

Aftercare: Bergenias

The leaf buds will start to push before the roots really get going, so don't be too impatient to pot them up. But once the roots are visible through the bottom of the tray tip the plantlets out carefully and, holding each one by the rhizome, pot it into a 9cm (3½in) pot of proprietary loam-based compost. Keep the rhizome on the surface of the compost and dress the pot with a handful of horticultural grit. Label each pot, retaining the master label with the batch, and water them thoroughly.

Pots of young bergenia plants can be kept outdoors throughout the growing season. They will need potting on into 1ltr (5in) pots by midsummer, and can be planted out in the autumn. It may be necessary to take some preventative measure against vine weevil with bergenias in pots (*see* section on Pests and Diseases in Part 3).

Bergenia *'Eric Smith'*.

Division of Bergenia rhizome

a)

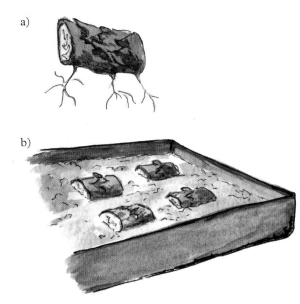

b)

a) Section of bergenia rhizome.
b) Bergenia sections positioned in contact with the compost.

Lily Division

Bulbils

Lilies that are growing in the ground or in pots will make small rooted bulbs alongside the main bulb after two or three years. These can be carefully lifted and grown on either in the garden or in pots of general compost (oriental lilies and their hybrids, however, need an acid soil or ericaceous mix compost).

Stem Bulbils

Some varieties produce bulbils on the flowering stem (tiger lilies are a well-known example). These enlarge while the plant flowers and start producing roots before dropping off to the ground. Again, they can be grown on in pots for about two years until they are flowering size and ready for the garden.

Scaling

So long as they are healthy and virus-free, lilies can also be propagated from their scales. These often detach themselves when you are digging them up or lifting the smaller bulbs. Half-fill a seed tray with general compost (or ericaceous mix if they are oriental lilies). Then spread a thin layer of horticultural sharp sand or fine grit over the surface. Gently push the scales, cut edge downwards into the sand, and when the tray is full work more sand in with your fingers until it covers all but the tips. Put the tray somewhere warm, about 10°C (50°F), and keep it just moist. Bulbils will form at the base of the scales and can be potted up the following spring. Pot them on each spring until they are flowering size and ready to plant out.

Bulbs and Corms

Growing on the offsets from bulbs and corms is simply a matter of detaching them, potting them up and waiting. Repot them every spring, or as soon as they make leafy growth and plant them out after about three to four years. Smaller offsets will clearly take longer than the larger ones.

However, bulbs, but not corms, can be cut up vertically from the tip through the basal plate when they are dormant. The basal plate of a bulb is a modified stem where the roots and leaves grow from, so if it is damaged in any way it will produce new buds or bulblets.

It is an agonizing technique. The temptation to use such a radical and risky method of propagation is only present in the impatient. Named, and very expensive, snowdrops are the usual victims to be eyed up. But to slice up a single bulb that has cost as much as a tree is a brave choice.

Cleanliness is next to carefulness when it comes to slicing up bulbs. Wear disposable gloves and sterilize a marble or glass chopping board, a sieve and your sharp knife with methylated spirits. Boil a kettle of water and let it go cold.

For each bulb, put about 350ml (12fl oz)of vermiculite into a clean bowl, add a little cooled, boiled water (about 30ml [1floz]) and leave it to imbibe. Mix up the smallest quantity of fungicide according to the manufacturer's instructions and pour some into a bowl.

Remove the brown skin from the bulb, leaving it white and shiny, and place it on the board. Trim the basal plate and cut off the top of the bulb, then wipe the cut surfaces with methylated spirits. Then cut the bulb in quarters vertically, making sure that each section is firmly attached to a piece of basal plate.

In the process of twin-scaling, the bulb is cut up further. Each section of basal plate has just two scales of the bulb attached. It's a delicate enterprise with a high risk of the scales dropping off the basal plate. Twin-scaling is, perhaps, best undertaken after a little experience.

The sections should then be dropped in a little of the fungicide solution and left for an hour. Put a little of the soaked vermiculite into a clear plastic bag, drain the bulb sections in the sieve and place them on a piece of kitchen towel to dry.

Then put one section at a time into the bag and shake each gently to cover it with vermiculite. The sections ought not to touch each other. Tie up the bag without blowing into it, label it with the name, date and number, then place it somewhere dark and warm like the airing cupboard. Check the bag regularly and if any sections have gone mouldy take them all out, discard the mouldy ones, repeat the fungicide procedure and use fresh vermiculite.

After about a month, the bulb scales will start to separate out and tiny bulbils should be forming on the basal plate. After about three months, the bulbils will be ready to pot up into new 10cm (4in) pots

Named Snowdrop cultivar.

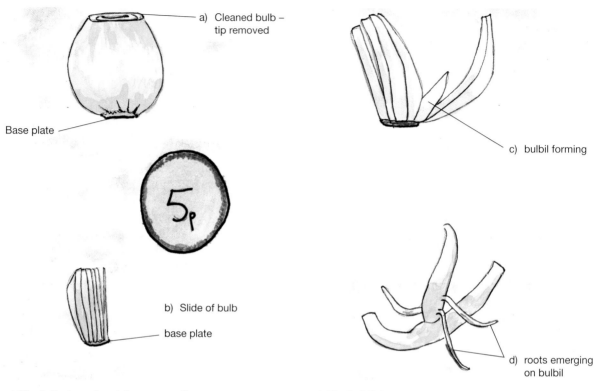

a) Cleaned bulb – tip removed

Base plate

b) Slide of bulb

base plate

c) bulbil forming

d) roots emerging on bulbil

a) The bulb cleaned and the top cut off.
b) The bulb sliced vertically with the basal plate attached.

c) The bulbil forming on the basal plate.
d) Roots emerging on the bulbil.

filled with general compost mixed 50:50 with vermiculite. Water them, label each pot and put them in a frost-free greenhouse for their first winter. They should produce leaves by spring and flower in a year or two.

DIVISION

Herbaceous perennials are plants that send up green flowering stems every summer, then die back down to a dormant crown in autumn and winter. The vast majority of these are easy to lift during the dormant season with a garden fork and the crowns split up into smaller plants. There is, however, one pitfall in particular awaiting the novice: that is, the problem of seeding into the crown. Named cultivars of a particular herbaceous plant, such as *Geranium pratense* 'Spinners', will not come true from seed (*see* Introduction); they will produce seedlings that are not,

A one-year-old bulbil.

by definition, *Geranium pratense* 'Spinners'. They will be different to their parent genetically. It follows that if you intend to divide a named cultivar, the seed heads must have been removed before they ripened in the summer.

Many hardy geraniums only flower once. Their faded flower heads can be cut off with a pair of shears to leave the basal rosette to clump up. Those that repeat will need shearing over more than once. It will be necessary to be a little more vigilant.

However, a few hardy geraniums do not make much of a crown. *Geranium* 'Salome', *G.* 'Anne Thompson' and *G.* 'Ann Folkard' among others grow from one or two overwintering buds to cover an area of about 1m (3ft 3in) in all directions and flower all summer. It is necessary to take cuttings of these and similar cultivars (*see* Softwood Cuttings on page 40).

Many plants, especially trees and hellebores produce a hormone in their roots that suppresses the growth of their own seedlings within their root run (*see* Introduction), but this is a limited factor that cannot be relied on. In the nursery trade, many herbaceous perennials are propagated by division without due care taken to dead-head the parent plants regularly. Astrantias in particular can be notoriously variable from seed. Discard the rogues in your garden and buy them in flower. If you want to divide them and produce plants that are true, you will have to dead-head them regularly.

Geranium *'Spinners'*.

When to Divide

Most herbaceous plants that die back in the winter to a dormant crown can be divided easily between November and March and the divisions replanted in the border. However, it is important not to lift and divide any plants if the weather is frosty or the ground is frozen. The water in the soil could freeze and kill the roots, and the soil will not settle back down among the roots properly, leaving air pockets that cause the roots to rot.

On heavy clay soils it is better to undertake this task in the spring when the soil is warming up rather than in November when the plants' roots are growing more slowly. They are less likely to make any headway into soggy soil that is already cooling down. It's a long time until the spring and in a cold, wet winter there is a danger that the roots will rot. If early winter is the only time available and the soil is heavy, mix in plenty of grit and garden compost around the roots. This will go some way to ameliorate the problem.

Conversely, if the soil is light and free-draining, November holds the promise of a long wet period. The roots can settle down into the soil and draw up plenty of winter moisture without any danger of rotting.

However, many garden soils are somewhere in-between the two extremes and on such soils the pragmatic way is to divide the herbaceous crowns while the border is being cleared and weeded, before a top dressing of organic matter is put down.

Astrantia major *'Shaggy'*.

Method

Lift the crown out of the ground with a border fork. Then, using a pair of forks, insert one across the middle of the crown. Push in the other fork next to the first, back to back, and separate the two halves by pulling the handles apart. This does less damage than using spades, although sometimes some plants need sharp stainless steel and spades or even a machete may prove necessary. Oriental hellebores, which do resent this barbarous treatment of their roots, certainly need more than a pair of forks.

The roots of creeping perennial weeds, such as couch grass and ground elder, often insinuate themselves into the root systems of herbaceous perennials. For this reason it is important to wash off the soil from the divided clumps so that you can spot any alien root systems. Docks and dandelions are easy to identify from their leaves and take out, root, leaves, stem and all. Couch grass roots are tough, thick, white and easily seen. Ground elder and mare's tail, on the other hand, have very brittle dark-coloured roots: and every tiny bit has the

b) Insert two forks back-to-back.

a) Lift the plant to be divided.

c) Pull the two handles apart . . .

d) . . . to separate the clump . . .

f) Lift the half, cleaned of any weeds and old growth. . .

e) . . . into two halves.

g) . . . and replant.

potential to regenerate. In borders that are infested with such pernicious weeds it would be wiser not to divide anything. Kill everything off and start again with newly bought plants at least a year later, once the border is totally clear of ground elder. Mare's tail is especially pernicious and almost impossible to eradicate totally.

Large clumps of herbaceous perennials often die from the middle out. Only the edges of the clump are actively growing. It is usually recommended to discard the central part of a large crown and only replant sections of the outer growth. It's for this reason that herbaceous borders should be dug up every five years or so and the plants split and replanted to reinvigorate them.

Aftercare

While the clumps are out of the ground dig in plenty of organic matter, such as well-rotted manure or garden compost. This will both absorb moisture for the roots and allow excess water to drain away. Replant the divisions, making sure that each new clump does not sit above the level of the surrounding soil, and water it in thoroughly. The soil will then be washed down amongst the roots without leaving large air pockets and will provide the plants with moisture at the outset.

When you have finished dividing and replanting, apply a mulch of organic matter for the worms to take down into the soil and open it up. This will also provide a slow release of nutrients once the plants start growing again.

Division of Ferns

Named ferns can be divided in late winter, just before they begin to push up their new fronds. It's a job that requires great care, as it's only too easy to end up destroying the mother plant. Lift the crown and tease the knobbly dormant growth apart, ensuring that each division has plenty of roots. Discard any knobs that break off without roots. Replant the divisions into improved soil.

Matteucia struthiopteris, the shuttlecock fern, is much easier, however. It runs quite vigorously if planted in moist shade. In late winter, cut the umbilical stems and lift the young ferns inde-

Unfurling crosiers of Matteucia struthiopteris.

pendently from the mother plant. They can be replanted into improved soil immediately.

Division of Ornamental Grasses

As a general rule, ornamental grasses should only be divided in the spring. They seem unwilling to settle down if they are divided in the autumn and have a propensity to rot in any soil. But by spring their roots are growing actively and the plant soon beds down and gets going.

Most species of grasses will produce plenty of seed, which germinates fast so that the resulting plants can be planted out at the end of the year they are sown or during the following spring. However, *Stipa gigantea* in particular seems to produce seed that is almost entirely sterile. Even though it does not bear a cultivar name, the only reliably successful way of propagating it is by division.

Method
If you plan to divide a named grass such as *Molinia caerulea* 'Transparent', it is important to cut off the

Stipa gigantea.

Young plants hardening off outside in late spring.

flowering heads before they set seed the previous summer. As with astrantias, this grass can seed back into the crown or its perimeter. Lift the entire plant with a fork and shake the surplus soil off. If the soil is particularly sticky, use a hose to wash it off so that you can see to separate out the individual plantlets. Try not to be too mean with these plantlets. If they are especially small or have very few roots they will quickly rot and die before they have had a chance to get going.

The plantlets can either be potted up and planted out later in the summer when they have made plenty of roots, or larger clumps that have merely been halved can be replanted into improved soil.

The dramatic, late-summer-flowering *Miscanthus sinensis*, however, does need a fair amount of brute force to dig up and divide, as they make very large root balls. It will take a hand axe to split them. Fortunately, their seed is only viable in the warmest parts of the country, so there is no problem of seeding into the crown. The whole operation, as with other grasses, should be undertaken in spring when their flowering stems are cut down.

GRAFTING AND BUDDING

Grafting is the technique of uniting the shoot of a named cultivar of a particular plant with the rootstock of another closely related plant. Budding is a form of grafting where only a single bud is used instead of a shoot.

Grafting and budding have been carried out, and the methods refined, over centuries. Once they were skills honed by every head gardener and inspired wonder and apprehension in every one of his trainees. These days, we are a little more knowledgeable about plants in general and propagation methods in particular, so we have greater success using other methods than in years gone by. Also, with the advent of successful micropropagation, many of those plants that were once grafted and budded are now propagated in laboratory conditions in large numbers. Consequently, in commercial horticulture grafting and budding are techniques that are used less and less, and are mostly confined to high-value shrubs that are propagated with limited success by other means; to top-fruit trees; and to roses. As a result, there are fewer people in the UK who have mastered the necessary skills

Wisteria floribunda '*Alba*' and Rosa '*Mme Léonie Viennot*'.

and can work fast enough than there were even twenty years ago. But for the enthusiast it remains a skilful and intensely satisfying method of propagation and manipulation of especially beautiful plants.

Reasons for Grafting and Budding

It can sometimes seem to the experienced gardener that the more attractive the plant is, the more difficult it is to propagate. Named cultivars of camellias, rhododendrons, magnolias, Japanese acers and certain conifers, for example, are notoriously difficult to root from cuttings. Commercially, a few of the more popular cultivars are micropropagated, but the more uncommon varieties in particular are still usually grafted onto seed-raised rootstocks. It's a more successful method if the only alternative is to take cuttings and the resulting plants are big enough to plant out more quickly. Also, it's a technique that with a bit of practice can prove very successful in amateur hands.

The rootstock is usually the common, easily grown, vigorous form of a slow-growing, perhaps rather weak, cultivar and lends its vigour to the plant being propagated: the scion. This is true in particular of roses and some named forms of Japanese acers. Alternatively, it is sometimes a lack of vigour, or a specific habit of growth, that is being imparted to the scion from the rootstock. Half a century of breeding rootstocks for fruit trees at the East Malling Research Station in Kent has resulted in a series of dwarfing rootstocks. This means that apples, pears, cherries and plums grafted onto these rootstocks will become low trees that are suitable both for commercial cropping by machine and for picking by hand by the gardener.

The rootstock can also impart disease-resistance to the scion. The Malling Merton apple rootstocks that were also developed at the East Malling Research Station are naturally resistant to woolly aphid, a common pest of apples commercially and in the garden. Roses are sometimes grafted onto rootstocks that tolerate a particularly low pH and onto others that are resistant to drought: another increasing problem in today's changing climate.

Perhaps of more interest to the amateur propagator is the technique of top-working small trees.

By grafting buds of a prostrate cultivar onto a root-stock at a height of, say, 1¾m (6ft), a weeping plant can be produced easily and relatively quickly. For instance, the weeping *Cotoneaster* 'Hybridus Pendulus' could be grafted at a height of, say, 1½m (5ft) onto a straight stem of *Cotoneaster bullatus* or *C.acutifolia* to create a dramatic weeping specimen plant. Or you could create your own standard roses by T-budding material from a small rambling rose such as *R.* 'Nozomi' onto a trained upright stem of a dog rose that has been raised from seed.

Family apple trees can be made by budding one or two different varieties onto an existing tree. Thus the one tree will produce two, three or more different sorts of apple; and thus the fruit from a single tree will be capable of cross-pollinating among the different varieties all growing on the same tree and occupying less space. Or a row of espalier-trained apples can be united where they meet by grafting one to the other. This makes the espalier stronger and more stable in the ground.

Materials Needed for Grafting and Budding

First and foremost you will need a strong, sharp knife. It is not absolutely essential that you use a specialist grafting or budding knife, but they do make the job easier if you plan to do a lot of this work. Keep your knife razor sharp with a whetstone: blunt knives are dangerous.

A pair of sharp secateurs that will make a clean cut is also important. Scissor-cut secateurs are always preferable to anvil-cut. You will also need old-fashioned raffia for tying up the graft. If this proves impossible to source, you could try using parcel tape and garden twine. Brown parcel tape is made of plastic which stretches and is waterproof. However, it is important to ensure that all the material at the point of union is absolutely dry when the tape is applied; also, if rain gets inside the tape can lose its stickiness and drop off. So a length of garden twine tied firmly over the top of the tape will help to keep it in position.

For bench-grafting acers and other special shrubs, you will need a frost-free greenhouse and a heated bench.

Budding and grafting knife with lip for lifting bark.

Felco secateurs with scissor cut.

Choice of Rootstock

The most important factor in grafting or budding any plant lies in the choice of the correct rootstock. It must be of the same genus as the scion or very closely related. Named cultivars of *Acer palmatum* and *A. japonicum*, for example, can be grafted onto *A. palmatum* that has been grown from seed. Witch hazels (*Hamamelis*) cultivars that are also difficult to root as cuttings can be grafted onto seed-raised *Hamamelis virginiana*, as can *Parrotia persica*, a very close relative to the witch hazels.

Over the years, certain species of a genus have been found to be more successful as rootstocks than others. Some rootstocks have proved to be too vigorous for the scion and suckering becomes a major problem in the garden. Sometimes the rootstock

COMPATIBLE ROOTSTOCKS FOR BENCH GRAFTING	
Genus of Scion	**Compatible Rootstock**
Abies	*Abies alba* *A. nordmanniana*
Acer palmatum and *A. japonicum*	*Acer palmatum*
Camellia cultivars	*Camellia japonica*
Chamaecyparis obtusa nana cultivars	*Chamaecyparis lawsoniana*
Cotoneaster hybridus pendulus	*Cotoneaster bullatus* *C. acutifolia*
Hamamelis cultivars	*Hamamelis virginiana*
Juniperus cultivars	*Juniperus virginiana*
Magnolia cultivars	*Magnolia kobus* *M. soulangeana*
Parrotia persica	*Hamamelis virginiana*
Picea cultivars	*Picea abies*
Pinus (two-needled) *Pinus sylvestris*	*Pinus* (five-needled) *P. strobus*
Rhododendron cultivars	*Rhododendron ponticum*
Rosa	*Rosa canina* (wild dog rose) *R. rugosa*
	R. multiflora
Syringa cultivars	*Syringa vulgaris* *S. tomentella*
Taxus cultivars	*Taxus baccata*
Thuja cultivars	*Thuja occidentalis*
Tsuga cultivars	*Tsuga canadensis*

variety bursts into spring growth well before the scion or *vice versa*. It can then be a problem to manage the plant. Cutting off all young growth from the rootstock could kill that rootstock before the scion has got moving. Or the scion could run out of stored energy if it tries to grow while the rootstock is still dormant.

Both the material for the rootstock and the scion need to be healthy and free from pests and diseases at the outset, for all the same reasons as cuttings material. They both need to be at roughly the same stage of growth. Ideally, the rootstock should be one season older at the point of union than the scion material and it is preferable that they are both roughly the same size. A union bulging out at an angle from the stem is unattractive and quite often vulnerable to knocks and bruises in the garden.

Incompatibility

In the period just after the Second World War, hybrid lilacs were very fashionable. Many new cultivars were bred in France with double flowers in all shades of white, pink and purple. However, at that time they were grafted onto ash or privet saplings. These are related to lilacs, but not closely enough. As a result, the graft union lasted a few years and then suddenly failed. The genetic incompatibility was too great. These days, the French hybrid lilacs are less popular and so less numerous, but they are grafted successfully onto *Syringa vulgaris*, the wild lilac, which is, of course, genetically much more closely related.

Very occasionally, a much older union will fail after ten or fifteen years, bringing a seemingly healthy tree crashing to the ground for no apparent reason. This is a particular problem in walnuts. The incompatibility manifests itself as a black line of dead tissue that encircles the tree at the union where the cells in the trunk have died. It is not known what causes this incompatibility.

More usually, if a union is going to fail it does so within its first year after grafting. The scion weakens and dies away from the rootstock. Sometimes the rootstock will start suckering vigorously: a portent of the failure of the scion. Or occasionally in the second year the plant will behave as if it's autumn. The leaves will start to colour in July or August and then the graft will start to fail. There is no easy cure. The simplest answer is to start again.

REMOVING GROWTH FROM BELOW THE UNION

Quite often, a young grafted plant, or one that has been stressed, will produce a shoot below the graft union from the rootstock. It is important that this sucker is cut off cleanly as soon as it has been noticed or the rootstock could take over from the scion, resulting in the graft failing.

a) Growth from the rootstock arising below the union on Acer *palmatum divisilobum.*

b) The graft union is visible above the sucker.

c) Cut the sucker off cleanly with the flat side of the secateurs' blade against the main stem . . .

d) . . . without leaving a snag.

Mostly it is skill with the knife at making clean, precise cuts that match up precisely on scion and rootstock that brings success. The cambium layer of cells just below the bark on the scion and the rootstock need to fuse together and unite, so the closer they come into contact the better the chances of the graft succeeding.

Timing

Grafting acers, conifers and special shrubs is one of those pleasant winter jobs that can be enjoyed in the shelter of the potting shed. The plants to be grafted together should be just coming into active growth in February or March. Any later in the spring and the sap will have started running and the wound, the union, will bleed out the excess sap. This can affect the scar tissue and prevent the wounds from healing.

Budding of shrubs and T-budding of roses is carried out in summer when the rind on the rootstock can be easily lifted to insert the bud. This is usually between July and September, preferably after a period of light rain, but not during a drought.

The whole process starts with the selection and growing on of the rootstocks. You may choose to start off two years earlier by sowing seed of *Chamaecyparis lawsoniana*, *Acer palmatum*, *Hamamelis* or *Magnolia*, for example. Or you might find seedlings in the garden that can be dug up and potted. Sometimes at plant fairs and flower shows up and down the country you can find nurserymen who will sell young saplings of acers or small seed-raised conifers. For the purposes of creating rootstocks the young plants need to be two years old and grown in 1ltr (5in) pots.

Bench Grafting

Bench grafting is so called because it is carried out on the propagating bench during the late winter. It can take several forms, but the most commonly used technique is the 'spliced side veneer graft'. Its name may sound complicated and it will take a bit of practice to master the technique, but it's probably the easiest and most successful graft to use on deciduous shrubs and conifers.

Choose healthy, straight-stemmed plants to make rootstocks for erect-growing cultivars and bent plants for prostrate or twisted specimens such as acers. Alternatively, it is possible to insert a length of wire and twist it gently around the still pliable stem. When you bend the stem to an angle it will harden and make wood in whatever shape you fancy. Remove the wire before it bites into the bark when the stem becomes woody. Grafting bent stems is much more difficult: keep the angle of the bent stem very wide. It is probably wise to tackle straight-stemmed grafts first.

About two months before grafting, bring the potted rootstocks into the greenhouse. If the roots are pushing out of the bottom of the pot, prune them with a pair of secateurs to encourage a good root system. Roots will branch when cut, just like the top growth. Water them well and keep them moist. About two weeks before grafting, stop watering them. This will reduce the flow of sap within the rootstocks and prevent them bleeding out from the grafting wound. The compost should be just moist: too dry or too wet will cause the graft to fail.

Before you start, sharpen your knife on a whetstone to ensure that you make all cuts with a clean, single stroke, then clean the blade with a dab of methylated spirits.

Prepare the rootstock by making a short downward cut across the stem, just above soil level. Then make a long cut, about 5cm (2in) down to meet the bottom of the lower cut. A sliver of rind can then be removed.

THE ROLE OF THE CAMBIUM LAYER IN GRAFTING

Not only does the cambium layer just beneath the skin produce roots in cuttings, it is also the part of the stem that forms the graft union. This is why it is vital that the two layers on the scion wood and the rootstock are in as close contact as possible. The less contact there is between the cambium layers, the more likely the graft will fail. Cambium does not occur in truly annual plants or in monocotyledonous plants. These cannot therefore be grafted.

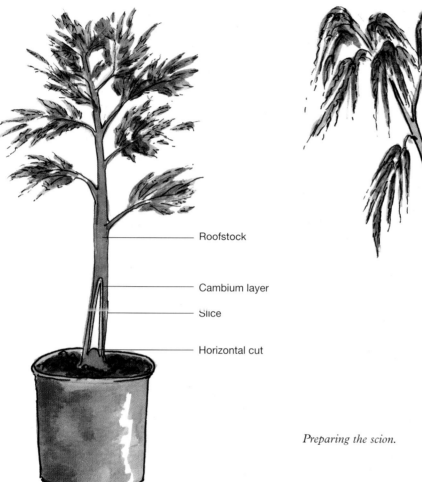

Preparing the rootstock.

- Roofstock
- Cambium layer
- Slice
- Horizontal cut

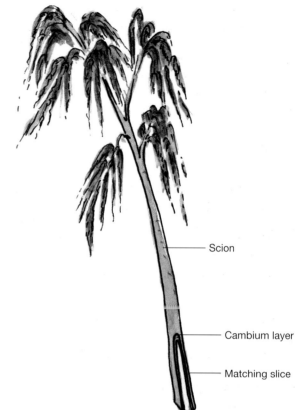

Preparing the scion.

- Scion
- Cambium layer
- Matching slice

Take the scion wood that has been removed from the mother plant, using healthy, well-ripened wood of the previous year's growth. (It can be stored if necessary in a plastic bag in the fridge.) It should be about a third the length of the rootstock. Make a 3–4cm (1¼–1½in) cut on the side opposite to the bud or shoot, so that it matches the cut on the rootstock exactly. Then make a very short angled cut on the opposite side at the base of the scion to form an angled point.

The scion should fit into the bottom notch on the rootstock and the cut edges should marry together precisely: the cambium layers need to grow together. It is essential that you don't touch the open wounds with your fingers.

Use raffia to bind the scion and rootstock together tightly, then tie it off neatly. This bandage will need to remain in place for several weeks.

The top growth of the rootstock is left in place and the pot plunged at an angle, the scion facing upwards, in a tray of moist peat (or peat substitute). The graft union should be clear of the peat. This is then placed on a heated bench with the thermostat set at 21°C (70°F). When you have completed the batch, cover the tray of grafts with a tent of clear polythene to retain the moisture at the site of the union. Open the tent regularly to disperse the condensation, watering the plants when and if is necessary.

After about four to six weeks, the top growth on the rootstock can be cut back by about a half, then

Fitting the scion onto the rootstock.

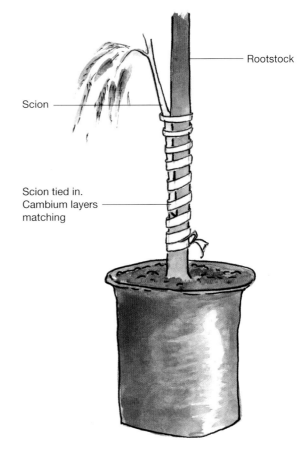

Binding the scion to the rootstock.

six weeks after that it can be removed altogether. At this stage, the binding raffia can be carefully cut off, taking care not to allow the knife to nick the skin. The finished plant is then gradually weaned out of the tent, into the greenhouse, and thence to a cold frame or polytunnel to grow away once all danger of frost has passed.

Uniting Espaliers

Growing fruit trees as espaliers is becoming increasingly popular. Espaliers are decorative, fruitful and take up less space than a conventional tree. Training espaliers is probably a job for the nurseryman,

but grafting two or three together to make a run of trees is something that any gardener can do successfully.

This is a job that is probably best undertaken in late winter/early spring, just before the trees come into active growth. Once the sap starts rising and the buds swell, there is the slight risk that the wounds will bleed and the graft will not take, although on apples and pears this is not such a major factor as it is with acers, for instance. It is even possible, but less successful, to make this graft at the time the espaliers are pruned in September.

Assuming the espalier-trained trees were planted at the same time and are the same age, their wood where the arms meet should be the same age and similar thickness. The method is technically called 'approach grafting' and it is by far the easiest form of grafting technique to undertake successfully.

a)

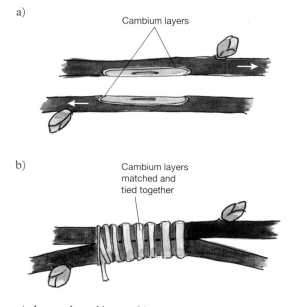

Cambium layers

b)

Cambium layers
matched and
tied together

a) Approach grafting: making matching cuts on each shoot
of an espalier.
b) Binding the graft firmly.

As the arms of the espaliers grow towards each other, tie them in straight on tight wires or canes so that they don't sag in the middle. Use shoots that were made the previous year and which are already growing horizontally. If you have to bend a shoot round it will always have an awkward bulge in the branch.

Take a long, elliptical, 3–4cm (1¼–1½in) slice, parallel to the shoot, removing a thin sliver of wood beneath the rind where each touches the other on the wire, without straining or bending the shoots. Make exactly the same size and shape cut on the other shoot. Squeeze the two together tightly, making sure the cambium layers are in precise contact, then bind them firmly with raffia.

Once the graft takes and both partners are growing away well, cut off the tips close to the union. If the graft has failed, cut the shoots back again to an outward-facing bud: it will be necessary to wait another year before trying again.

Budding

It can be fun to create family fruit trees where one tree has other cultivars budded onto the crown to produce different apple or pear varieties on the same tree. This technique is best carried out in July and August when the trees are in active growth and the sap is flowing, as the bud will be accepted more quickly. As mentioned before, apples and pears bleed much less than subjects such as acers, which have to be grafted in the dormant season. However, if the weather is very wet or there is a drought it is best to wait for conditions to return to normal.

Select a well-branched young fruit tree that was planted during the previous winter to act as the rootstock, the parent tree. However, you will be leaving at least one of its shoots to provide its own fruit and not cut off all the top growth as if it was merely a rootstock. Then cut young half-ripe shoots of the current year's growth from the scion trees to be grafted onto the parent. Remove the leaves to prevent any loss of moisture, leaving the leaf stalks, the petioles, intact to pick up and insert the buds.

Select a bud on the scion wood below the top three buds which should not be used. These are usually flower buds that will not make leafy growth. Holding the shoot with the buds facing towards you, make a long, shallow cut 1cm (⅓in) below the chosen bud, slicing underneath, parallel to the

a)   b)

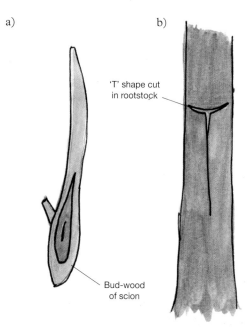

'T' shape cut
in rootstock

Bud-wood
of scion

a) The bud on the scion wood.
b) A 'T'-shaped cut on the rootstock.

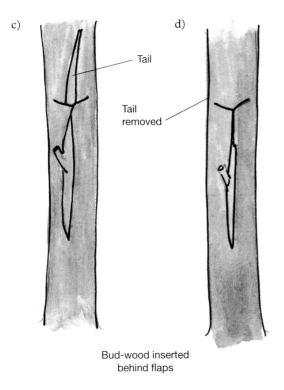

c) Insert the bud.

d) The tail trimmed off and the bud ready to be tied in.

shoot, so that the bud is removed with a thin sliver of wood beneath. Cut off the tip of the rind at the base. If the wood is too thick it can be carefully removed from the rind containing the bud. This is a very difficult thing to do, however, and it may be wiser to start again with another bud.

On the parent wood acting as the rootstock, make a 'T'-shaped cut in the rind of a shoot of similar size at the height required. Ideally, choose a position to the leeward side of the tree to prevent the prevailing wind from blasting and drying out the scion bud before it has had a chance to take. Start with the horizontal cut, then make a vertical cut about 3cm (1¼in) long to make the stem of the 'T'. If you have a budding knife use the tongue to lift the flaps

of bark on the shoot formed by the T-cut and ease the bud right in, holding it by the leaf petiole. Then tie it in firmly with raffia.

The bud will remain dormant until the following spring. If the leaf petiole drops off, this is usually a sign that the bud has taken. Before growth starts in the spring, carefully remove the raffia if it has not already dropped off, taking care not to nick the rind. Then cut off the shoot of parent wood with a pair of sharp secateurs just above the bud and tie in the new shoot with a length of garden twine or raffia, to a cane or another shoot on the parent tree. At one time, the old head gardeners would leave a snag of parent wood to use as a support, but there is a risk of the snag dying back into the graft.

This method can also be used to top-work trees such as cotoneaster or roses. Use at least three buds, preferably five if possible, to allow for some failures. If only one or two buds succeed, the top-worked tree will need some expert pruning if it is not to appear unbalanced.

Aftercare

Once a graft has taken and the new scion is growing away well, plant the new tree or shrub in the usual way with lots of garden compost or well-rotted manure in the planting hole and keep it watered. Make sure that the point of union of the graft is above soil level.

Prune it correctly as you would any other shrub or fruit tree and remove any suckers that arise from below the union on the rootstock. They will quickly take over the weaker scion. Suckers should be removed as close to the stem or roots as possible to prevent them from regrowing.

Top-worked shrubs and roses are greatly enhanced by tying them in, at least initially, to a prefabricated, umbrella-shaped frame. Roses, in particular, will produce more flowers from shoots that are tied down than from those that grow straight up.

PART 3

Practicalities of Propagation

PESTS AND DISEASES

There can be few things more dispiriting to a propagator than to see all that work destroyed, sometimes overnight, by the army of pests and diseases that seem to be out there just waiting their chance. Sometimes it can seem thoroughly daunting. Sometimes it is. But pests and diseases have natural cycles of population or infection. Some years the combination of weather conditions is favourable to a particular pest or fungus; in other years less so. Populations of pests in particular do vary from year to year. We all remember years when there seem to have been swarms of ladybirds (which are not pests at all), or years when there were no wasps (which are not all bad really).

This book does not set out only eco-friendly, green solutions, but trying to resolve problems without recourse to chemicals in the garden is always wise. Not only does the population of predators increase in relation to the availability of prey, but also that prey will eventually produce a generation that is resistant to the chemical if it is used repeatedly. So if the only recourse is to insecticides and fungicides, buy a different brand with a different active chemical constituent every time. It will go some way to preventing the build-up of resistance to a particular pesticide in your garden if there is no other method.

Pests and Diseases of Seedlings

Pests and diseases are more common, more easily spread and more devastating within the enclosed warm spaces between seedlings. Good hygiene is the most important safeguard and vigilance against any sign of pest attack is vital.

Birds
Everyone loves garden birds. They are part of the reason for having a garden. However, birds do have some bad habits. A particular problem in a dry spring is that birds take up beaks-full of watered seed compost, with a side-dressing of newly germinated seedlings, and squeeze the water out of them. The result is total destruction of a tray of long awaited hellebores or primroses. Put a net over any seed trays that are germinated out of the greenhouse.

Damping Off
Seedlings are most at risk of the fungal rot commonly called damping-off disease. A patch appears where newly emerged seedlings have keeled over and become black. It will spread within hours and soon demolish the whole crop.

To prevent seedlings from damping off, sow the seed thinly to allow plenty of ventilation when they germinate, especially where the stalks meet the compost. Seedlings should also be given plenty of light to prevent them getting tall and etiolated, softer and more susceptible. A chemical fungicide drench such as Cheshunt Compound, if it is available, can also be watered on when the seed is sown and when the seedlings are pricked out.

Mice
Hellebore seeds are a particular delicacy for mice during a long autumn and winter while the seeds are stratifying in a pot outside. Nets go some way to preventing their attentions, but you may have to use mousetraps if they are persistent.

Sciarid Fly
These can be a problem when peat-based composts are used. The adults are black, about 4mm (⅛in)

long and jump about on top of the containers. Their tiny white larvae are just visible on the surface of the compost and can attack the stems of seedlings. The easiest remedy is to pot up the seedlings, cleaning off and discarding the top, infected layer of compost. A permethrin-based spray after the seedlings have been watered in is usually sufficient to effect a permanent cure. Sciarid flies rarely return once the pots have left the moist warmth of a greenhouse.

Slugs and Snails

Slugs and snails particularly relish plants in frames and greenhouses and can devour a tray or two of seedlings in a night. If you have no moral objections, slug pellets can be put down under the pots and trays, hidden from view. They are coloured blue to make them invisible to birds. These days, most are non-toxic to other animals, but, to be sure, avoid them, especially if you have dogs. They don't ask questions first. The alternatives are many and various, both chemical and non-chemical. Slug pubs are effective, although some would argue that alcohol is a worse chemical than metaldehyde.

Pests and Diseases of Cuttings

Some pests and diseases are more of a problem for plants at the cuttings stage than they are when those mature plants are growing away vigorously in the garden. Start with cuttings taken from healthy material that is free from pest and disease at the outset. As stated before, the warmth and moisture of a greenhouse is heaven on earth for every bug and fungus in your garden.

One way to monitor what pests are inhabiting the greenhouse is to hang up yellow sticky papers that are available from the garden centres. Examine them closely every day or two to spot aphids and whiteflies. Needless to say, remove them if you decide to use predatory insects as biological controls.

Aphids

Adult greenfly and, less commonly, blackfly are easy to spot, their eggs less so. The sloughed skins of the nymphs are white, but are of course completely stationary (unlike whitefly, which fly off at a touch).

Aphids suck the sap of a plant, weakening and distorting its growth and potentially transmitting virus diseases from one plant to another. Most types are specific to their hosts, although some are less fussy. They are very difficult to get rid of. The wisest course of action on the propagation bench is to throw out all affected cuttings and spray the remainder with an effective remedy. There are plenty of them on the market, both organic and chemical. And be vigilant for at least two weeks thereafter.

Eelworm

This microscopic worm is endemic to Japanese anemones, border phlox and penstemons. Each eelworm species is specific to its host. That is, phlox eelworm will not infect Japanese anemones and penstemons and *vice versa*. Although they are microscopic, the infected plants will visibly have twisted brown leaves at the base and after two or three years they will die right back. Eelworms infect the stems and leaves of their hosts, but not the roots. Happily, it is possible to take root cuttings of Japanese anemones and border phlox, but, alas, named penstemons can only be propagated by softwood cuttings of the stem. Although it is possible for penstemons to outrun and outgrow the eelworms when they are growing fast, early in the summer, it is still taking a chance to propagate even from the top shoots. The answer is to buy new, clean plants from the garden centre or nursery. These have been cleaned up in recent years through the process of micropropagation.

Eelworm can be spread by contaminated secateurs and knives, and their eggs can survive in the soil for years without a host, so it is important not to replace the same plant in the same position. There is nothing that can eradicate them at present.

Fungal Diseases

Damping off, botrytis and other moulds occur most commonly among cuttings whenever and wherever the conditions are damp. This can occur where leaves touch each other, the container, the plastic bag or tent. Ensure that there is enough space between the cuttings; plenty of air flow; and don't cram too many in a single pot. Prevention is better than cure. Remove any dead cuttings and any dropped leaves immediately and spray with a copper-based fungicide if it is available and you have no moral objection.

When rhizomes or root cuttings are made that expose a large cut surface area to potential fungal infection, it is wise to apply a dusting of green sulphur powder, if it's available. A wet fungicidal solution is not practical.

Leatherjackets
These are the larvae of daddy longlegs, or craneflies, that are a particular problem in pots that are standing outside during a wet winter. The grubs are large in both size and appetite and eat the roots of young plants, especially if the compost is too wet.

When the pots are being moved in the autumn to their winter quarters it is wise to remove the top centimetre (⅓in) of compost, especially if it is covered in moss or liverwort. Quite often, the grubs will be hiding under their mossy blanket with food on tap all winter, ready to hatch in spring.

Mice
Mice are especially fond of bulbous plants and are a particular problem in the autumn with the first frosts. They are looking for a snug winter nest, again fully catered. Humane mouse traps are effective, but need visiting every day. Twenty-four hours is a long time to an imprisoned mouse.

Red Spider Mite
Red spider mite (RSM) is microscopic and not to be confused with perfectly visible little brick-red spiders. RSM live on the underside of the leaves, quietly munching away at the green chlorophyll. The infected leaves are therefore noticeably more yellow in patches, eventually shrivelling up and dropping off. In a severe infestation, the RSM will even weave webs among the leaves.

They are very difficult to eradicate and any suspicion of RSM infestation should prevent all propagation of infected plants. Although RSM is a pest of greenhouses and polytunnels, they can and do invade the garden in a warm, dry summer. They are an increasing problem due not only to climate change, but also to their resistance to insecticides. The biological control, the predatory mite *Phytoseiulus persimilis*, is effective within the contained environment of a greenhouse. Otherwise, the best recourse is to destroy all the infected plants before the RSM spreads further.

Scale Insect
These are a form of hard-shelled aphid that lock onto the underside of evergreen shrub leaves and stems, sucking the sap in typical aphid-manner. They are very damaging to young plants in particular. They can be sprayed with a chemical specific to scale insects that penetrates their hard shells; or, if you have the time and inclination, on a small plant they can be squashed with your thumbnail.

Sciarid Flies
These can appear on the surface of the compost while cuttings are rooting, but unless they and their larvae are especially numerous they are less of a pest on cuttings than seedlings. They can affect cuttings with small leaves, such as heathers or lavenders, especially if these are kept too damp. Long-term cuttings of evergreens are less susceptible as they are grown at a colder time of year. Sciarid flies tend to disappear when the cuttings are potted up and the surface layer of soil is discarded.

Slugs and Snails
Just as with seedlings and fully mature plants, slugs and snails can devastate trays of cuttings (*see* above for methods of control).

Sooty Mould
Aphids are also responsible for the appearance of sooty mould on shrubs, especially evergreens. Greenfly exude a sticky sap called honeydew which attracts the spores of sooty mould. The leaves quickly look as if they have been dusted with the eponymous soot, which is easily wiped off with finger and thumb. However, practically speaking, the remedy is to spray the shrub with an aphicide. Apply a little fertilizer if the treatment has been done before July and the shrub will simply grow out of the mould.

Vine Weevil
This is perhaps the major pest at the potting stage. The adults are dark grey-black, have pointed snouts and their feet turned out like Charlie Chaplin in hobnail boots. They should not to be confused with fast, shiny black beetles: the latter are the good guys. Adults take half-moon-shaped bites out of the edge of leaves. This may be a bit disfiguring, but it is a useful calling card. Vine weevils are about, if not in residence.

Then the adults, without the intervention of a partner, lay their eggs right into the middle of the

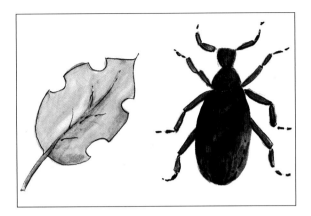

Adult vine weevil.

crown of a plant where the stems meet the soil. They hatch out into comma-shaped creamy white larvae with brown heads. These are the guys that do the damage. They and their cohorts set about munching their way through the plant's entire root system. The leaves of the plant consequently droop in the pot. A quick tug soon reveals the absence of any roots. At the next stage, the larvae develop into creamy white versions of the adult, curled up among all that is left of the roots until eventually they pupate into adults. They are particularly fond of primula, heuchera, tiarella, bergenia, saxifraga, geum, epimedium, rhododendrons and camellias. However, they will try anything if they are desperate. They dislike life in loam-based compost and are less of a menace outside in the garden. There are all sorts of preventatives on the market, both chemical and biological controls, for use on containers.

Whitefly

Whiteflies are tiny, with triangular wings, and rise up at the slightest touch of an infected leaf. They are very bad news among cuttings: to be avoided at all costs. Their eggs appear as a slight white haze on the underside of a leaf. But even if you are careful to avoid infected cutting material, during a warm, dry spell whiteflies have no compunction about flying in through the greenhouse window and laying their eggs, especially on fuchsias and pelargoniums. Salvias, solanums and perennial nasturtiums are also particularly prone to their attentions. Tomatoes are also vulnerable if you grow them in the greenhouse in the summer. Celandines, milk thistle and milkweed act as hosts for whitefly eggs during the winter. Make sure these weeds are completely eradicated from the garden.

If any cutting or plant in the greenhouse is found to be affected, take a very large plastic bag and quietly draw it over the plant. Tie it up at the neck and put bag, plant and all in the bin. Then begin the treatment.

Whiteflies are particularly difficult to eradicate, as they pupate through several stages before they fly. As the earlier stages are unaffected by sprays, they need treating every five days for up to seven weeks before they are under control. Alternatively, biological controls are useful. *Encarsia formosa* is a little wasp that can be ordered from specialist companies. Their main drawback, however, is that they tend to fly out of the greenhouse window.

Virus Diseases

Viruses in plants are as hard to diagnose as they are in small children. They produce a wide range of symptoms and are completely without a cure. Generally, virus infection distorts the leaves and flowers. They may be mottled or streaked, and the plant's growth may be yellow, contorted and weak. Any one of these symptoms could also be the result of a nutritional deficiency, so it's worth trying to remedy that first if the plant is particularly precious. Otherwise, the only recourse is to dig it up and bin or burn it. Do not put it on the compost heap.

Viruses are transmitted either by sap-sucking insects, such as whitefly and aphids, or on your secateurs or knife, so if a plant is infected, spray the remaining plants of the same genus against aphids and whitefly. Clearly, it is important not to take cuttings from a diseased plant.

If you do suspect the presence of a virus in a plant, it should be destroyed. But if there is only a faint suspicion and the plant is particularly precious, leave the sickling *in situ* but spray all the plants of the same genus in the neighbourhood. Keep a watchful eye on the sick plant and if the symptoms worsen, remove it at once and bin or burn it. Clean your knife and secateurs with methylated spirits thoroughly if they have accidentally come into contact with a diseased plant.

Weeds

Weeds are not just the bane of the gardener's life, they are more than a nuisance when they grow in potted seedlings and cuttings. They rob the young plant of nutrients and moisture. They sometimes carry pests and diseases that can be transmitted to the plants. And they drop their seeds back down into the pot ready to re-emerge at the next stage of the plant's growth.

For these reasons, it is important to keep on top of any weeds that appear in pots of young plants. When plants are being repotted, remove the top layer of compost and discard it. Even if it has no weeds visible, the seeds are often just on the surface waiting their chance.

If one or two pots in a batch of young plants have an especially thick crop of weeds, it is likely that those plants are struggling or dying. The weeds are growing well because the plant is not taking up the nutrients.

All the usual suspects in your garden can move house into pots of delicious fresh compost, but the following are probably the worst and may well be endemic in the compost you are using:

- *Hairy bittercress* is one of the most common and difficult to eradicate. It has small white flowers and seed pods that explode everywhere. This annual weed is able to flower and set seed many times throughout the year. Try to remove it before it even thinks of flowering.
- *Goat willow* is another insidious invader. Its slim, woody seedlings grow very fast and can become small trees within a summer, even in a pot. When they are removed at a late stage, the original occupant has often shrivelled and died in the shadow of this cuckoo in the pot.
- *Annual meadow-grass* is another deep-rooted cuckoo that quickly robs the young plant of nourishment. Remove it as early as possible, before the roots travel down and enclose the plant's roots in their greedy clutches.
- *Moss and liverworts* are the bane of every propagator. Either will form a thick green mat on the surface of the pot and, if it is not removed, it will creep across the pot rim to invade the neighbours. Liverwort, in particular, occurs mostly when plants are being irrigated by an overhead spray. It absorbs the water, causing the young plants' roots to come up to the surface to seek moisture. And if the plants are standing outside in pots, liverwort welcomes the attentions of Daddy Longlegs, or cranefly, who lay their eggs under the surface mat. Moss and liverwort can be lifted off the surface of the pot like a carpet, but they take about 1cm (⅓in) of soil with them and the pot will need to be topped up with compost or grit. Once the plants are out in the garden border, the liverwort will usually disappear unless the ground is particularly badly drained.

TOOLS AND EQUIPMENT

It's perfectly possible to spend a small fortune on special equipment and gadgets to aid propagation, but whereas the gadgets can be useful eventually, it is the basics that are important to get right at the outset. It's wiser to spend as much money as is affordable on these, rather than skimp in order to buy some of the extras. As in all things, you get what you pay for.

The Greenhouse

Perhaps the biggest and most expensive piece of equipment is a greenhouse. Throughout this book, it has not been assumed that a greenhouse is essential. It is not. However, the alternative cool windowsills and porches have their limitations of space, temperature and cleanliness. Not everyone wants to sleep in a spare bedroom full of burgeoning pansies, soil and greenfly. And a porch full of trays of seedlings is vulnerable to small children, flying Wellingtons and wet dogs. So a greenhouse is well worth saving up the pocket money for if you want to do some serious propagation. It may be hard to argue a case for it in economic terms, but as a hobby it is cheaper than golf, fishing or shopping.

A well-maintained greenhouse will provide the ideal climate for nurturing seedlings and cuttings. It will protect the youngsters from the extremes of

Potting up in late spring.

weather: wind, heavy rain and a few degrees of frost without any extra heating. Above all, you, the propagator, will be able to control the temperature, moisture levels and light.

Of course, so will a polytunnel, albeit to a lesser extent. However, a greenhouse, or that should be a glasshouse, is just that: made of glass, and glass wins out over plastic in all respects, except cost. Glass allows the Sun's ultraviolet rays in to warm everything within the greenhouse, such as paved paths, soil, the benches or staging, and of course the plants. Then, because infrared radiation (that is, heat) is much slower to pass out again through glass, the greenhouse retains that heat, warming the air near the ground. The plastic sides of a polytunnel allow the infrared radiation to travel out again immediately, so the air temperature inside the polytunnel will cool quickly. Therefore, heating a greenhouse, or keeping the air temperature a few degrees above freezing, is a viable proposition, while heating a polytunnel is not.

Choosing a Greenhouse

There are so many makes of greenhouses on the market that it's hard to choose the right one. The truth is that they are all just as good as each other, but there are some factors that will help you to choose which one is appropriate to your needs. Other than cost, the most important factor is size and space. Choose the largest size that you can afford and for which you have room in the garden. Like kitchen cupboards, greenhouses are always too small: as your enthusiasm for propagation grows, the greenhouse space contracts. However, it also follows that the larger the internal space, the more it will cost to keep it frost-free. Running costs always escalate, although there are ways round this problem.

Siting

A greenhouse ideally should be situated in the sunniest part of the garden, well away from any trees that might shade it. But often compromises have to be made. Loss of light should be balanced against protection from the prevailing wind. Gales and high winds can cause damage from flying fruit, branches or worse. Once a pane of glass has been broken, the wind can get inside the greenhouse and wreak havoc or even explode it. A hedge, trellising with climbers or, less decoratively, plastic windbreak material will all slow the wind speed down without causing turbulence. Solid walls and fences, on the other hand, present an impenetrable barrier to the wind, which will then swoop upwards and over the top, causing mini-whirlwinds on the side of the greenhouse. All windbreaks will cut down the light to some extent.

Try to position the greenhouse away from any frost pockets in the garden. These are not immediately obvious in a newly purchased house until a few frosts have demonstrated the coldest areas. Often they are at the bottom of a hill, where the frost rolls down only to collect in your new greenhouse. Or they may be in a low-lying dip in the land. This might flood too and bring more hazards to your new greenhouse and its contents.

In an average back garden, however, there tend to be very few options. Traditionally, the greenhouse sits at the end of the garden, screened off from the lawns and flowerbeds, surrounded by the vegetable patch and out of sight. However, this template is

An attractive greenhouse or conservatory.

A conventional greenhouse with a pitched roof.

changing with the advent of some very decorative greenhouses that would adorn the most immaculate garden.

Positioning an attractive greenhouse near the back of the house has some distinct advantages. It would be a much more enjoyable prospect on a cold, wet winter's day to nip into the greenhouse and get on with the root cuttings, than to traipse down a long muddy path to the end of the garden. Installing power to the greenhouse for the heating and, possibly, lighting would be much easier and cheaper than running a subterranean cable the length of the garden. The further away the greenhouse is from the domestic power supply, the more power is lost. Also, unless you plan to live in a greenhouse at the end of the garden all day, it is much easier to keep an eye on the watering and ventilation when it is within view of the rear house windows.

Domestic greenhouses do not usually need planning permission, but check with the local Planning Department first to be on the safe side.

Shape

The conventional rectangular shape of a greenhouse with a pitched roof has few faults, providing the eaves are at a comfortable height above the staging. You will be able to choose whether to have glass to the ground to maximize the amount of light and ventilation at floor level, or a low wall. The latter can be useful for building cold frames adjacent to the greenhouse, but it does rob the light from under the staging and leads to poor air circulation at ground level, causing the build-up of fungal disease.

If the only option is to site a greenhouse where it is vulnerable to wind, there are semi-dodecagon or arch-shaped greenhouses available. By presenting the side of the arched greenhouse to the wind, the passage of air will travel harmlessly over the top without interruption. The perpendicular walls of a conventional greenhouse would face the wind full-on and be more susceptible to damage. Semi-dodecagon greenhouses also offer the optimum area of glass in a given area: they have no internal supports and plenty of headroom.

Geodesic dome-shaped greenhouses really maximize the light and space available. They are very strong structurally and offer the potential for very even ventilation. If your garden can take it, their angular looks are modern and attractive in the right place.

An arch-shaped greenhouse.

A lean-to greenhouse.

Another alternative to consider is a lean-to greenhouse on a south- or west-facing wall. If you have the appropriate space, such a building would enjoy the radiated heat of the house wall on cold nights and need much less heating. The plants further from the wall could be covered with horticultural fleece on particularly frosty nights or in extremely cold areas of the UK. However, if a lean-to greenhouse covers a house or garage doorway, the glazing must conform to British Standard regulations regarding toughened glass.

Materials

A classic greenhouse is constructed of cedar wood, which is durable and slow to rot. The timber should come from a managed source. Cedar wood is more expensive than the alternatives, but has natural good looks, better heat retention and is often stronger than aluminium. And it has a lovely scent.

Greenhouses are often constructed on a low wall, which makes an ideal backing to a cold frame, but, as mentioned above, it does reduce the light and ventilation at ground level.

The cheapest materials used to construct a greenhouse are either extruded aluminium or folded alloy sheeting. They need no maintenance apart from cleaning when the moss collects in the cracks, but they do look functional rather than attractive. The glass is held in place in aluminium alloy greenhouses with spring clips, which might be a problem on a windy site. The glass in extruded aluminium-framed greenhouses is held in place by bar-capping or glazing caps, which are actually screwed into the framework, therefore making the greenhouse much stronger, albeit costlier.

An expensive extra that should be considered is toughened glass. These days, all manufacturers offer this option, which is especially important if there are children or bouncy dogs in the garden. And it is frighteningly easy to use ladders near panes of glass. Ordinary horticultural glass makes large, lethal splinters, while toughened glass shatters like a car windscreen into thousands of granules. It should meet the BS6206 Class A standard.

Guttering and downpipes are usually integral, but it's worth checking if they are configured to drain

A cedar-wood greenhouse.

Wooden greenhouse constructed on a low wall.

Cold frames against the low wall.

into a water butt for irrigating the garden (but not seedlings and cuttings).

Ventilation

Adequate ventilation is essential for raising young plants successfully. More cuttings and seedlings are lost through fungal disease than from any other cause. Keeping the air moving reduces high temperatures and humidity, thus helping to prevent the build-up of fungal spores on and around the plants, the staging and inside the glass. The ventilation that comes as standard on most makes of domestic greenhouse is not adequate for this task.

Ventilation is provided through the door, roof vents, windows and louvred side panels just above ground level. Adding some extra windows and louvres when you order your greenhouse from the manufacturer will be worth every penny extra.

If you are away during the day, it might be worth investing in automatic vent openers. In comparison with the cost of the greenhouse they are not that expensive. They consist of a wax-filled piston connected to an arm fixed to the frame of the greenhouse and the vent or window. As the temperature rises, the wax expands, pushing the piston upwards so that the vent or window opens, and *vice versa*. They usually operate above a temperature of 10°–15°C (50°–59°F).

Alternatively, an electrician could fit an extractor fan, providing the greenhouse has a power supply. A glazier would also need to cut a hole in the glass. But a good extractor fan will change the air in a small greenhouse every three or four minutes and can be controlled by a thermostat.

Floor Surface

There are two basic options for the floor of your greenhouse: a concrete base or bare earth. Either way, the floor must be level. The choice depends on the style of greenhouse and advice should be sought about preparing the site.

From the user's point of view there is surprisingly little difference. A concrete floor will be easy to sweep, keep clean and damp down. It will be easier to keep weed-free, although pests and diseases will find nooks and crannies anyway. But it would be more time-consuming, labour intensive and expensive to make. Bare earth, on the other hand, is the easy option. It tends to come with its own flora and fauna of weeds, pest and disease, but these are soon knocked on the head with regular attention and good hygiene. If the earth is covered in a permeable membrane and topped with horticultural grit, it will drain off excess moisture well when the greenhouse is being watered. A simple flagstone path can be laid up the middle.

Installation

Greenhouses are nowadays manufactured for self-assembly, with the exception of the more decorative models. If you are daunted at the prospect of DIY, and there are no odd-job men in the neighbourhood, the manufacturers are usually able to recommend someone. However, there is always a comprehensive instruction booklet included and with patience and common sense it is not a difficult job for the able-bodied: preferably two able-bodied.

Staging

There's still the small matter of erecting the staging. It's best if you buy it from the same greenhouse manufacturer and it's delivered at the same time, as it will then fit exactly and match the style of the greenhouse: aluminium or cedar wood.

Staging is an essential extra for the propagator. It offers the potential of a shady, but not dark, area beneath as well as a sunny bench on top.

Capillary Matting

A sheet of capillary matting on top of the staging will act as a moist sponge, holding the water and creating a humid atmosphere for the plants sitting on top. As the compost in the pots dries, it draws up moisture from the matting until that too has dried out. It therefore acts as a safety reservoir on a sunny day. In addition, it can be used as a self-watering system. One end of the matting can be immersed in a container of water so that moisture is continually drawn up like a wick. However, on particularly sunny or windy days the young plants will probably still need additional irrigation from a hose or watering can. A disadvantage of the capillary system is that as the plants' roots grow out of the

Small staging and potting bench.

bottom of the pots, they grow into the matting. If a pot is picked up, the roots will be severed and the plant will need immediate repotting. Roots are less likely to grow into capillary matting that is not kept immersed, but allowed to dry out periodically.

Electric Power Supply

A power supply is required for fan-heating the greenhouse in winter, for a bench heater and for propagators. It is also needed for a mist unit and for lighting if you anticipate working after dark. However, all these things do have alternatives: a paraffin or propane gas heater would be good alternatives to an electric fan-heater; and the remainder are useful but optional.

Any electrical work should always be carried out by a qualified electrician, who will fit the correct cabling and outdoor watertight power sockets inside the greenhouse. It may be necessary to dig an underground trench to the greenhouse for the cabling and an electrician will advise you of the minimum statutory depth. Lengths of overhead cables are extremely hazardous in a garden and should only be used for very short distances.

Irrigation

There are all manner of automatic watering systems that could be installed if you plan to be away from the greenhouse for any length of time. There are drip systems where the nozzle of a small pipe is inserted into each pot or container. They need checking regularly to make sure they are kept clear and not blocked by fungus, limescale or soil particles. Or you could install micro-drip low sprayers along the bench to stand between the pots. The sprayers can also be further adapted by connecting them to an automatic timer, which switches the water on at regular intervals or maybe at 2.00am every summer night. They use less water than sprays or hoses, but the connections need to be very tight and secure. It's disastrous to return from a holiday to a greenhouse full of dead plants and a running tap where the connection has burst. Ask a friendly neighbour to pop in to check it regularly; also, water sprays out in a circular disc shape, so there are always corners left dry that will need regular hand-watering.

That friendly neighbour, on the other hand, might be persuaded to turn on an overhead spray line connected to the greenhouse frame every evening instead. However, not only are there still going to be a few dry spots, but this method is far more wasteful of water as moisture is lost to evaporation. On balance, it is more economic of water and time to use a low-pressure hose by hand so that you can direct the water where it is needed underneath the leaves and onto the compost. But that might be asking too much of your neighbour when you are away.

Misting

If you plan to do lots of summer propagation it might be worth looking into connecting up a mist unit. This would require a constant and secure source of water, plus a power supply.

A series of nozzles on 30cm (1ft) high pipes sprays a light mist over the cuttings, keeping them permanently turgid, that is, full of moisture. It is controlled by an electronic artificial leaf. This is a moisture sensor connected to a control box. The leaf is positioned amongst the cuttings. When the leaf is dry, the control box causes the solenoid valve to open and allow water into the mist pipes and nozzles. The mist is sprayed for a set length of time: twenty or thirty seconds is usual. The artificial leaf is moistened along with its real neighbours until it dries out again. It is not normally necessary to have this switched on at night in the UK. In summer the whole unit is usually contained under a plastic tent to prevent faster evaporation.

Heating

Before deciding how best to heat your greenhouse, first consider insulating it in the winter. Bubble-plastic Heatsheets are a cheap and simple way to reduce fuel consumption. They are UV-stabilized and can be bought in continuous lengths ready to cut to shape as required. The standard widths allow an overlap for easy fixing to the glazing bars of the greenhouse with special clips. They should last for two or three seasons if they are handled carefully, although it might be wiser to start afresh each winter to ensure that there are no residues of pest and disease trapped in the Heatsheet.

The vast majority of cuttings need only to be kept frost-free. They do not need high temperatures. Nor does the entire greenhouse have to be kept frost-free. It is possible to buy an internal partition to make a separate heated inner sanctum, thus saving on heating bills. There are also plug-in propagators of all sizes that will achieve the same ends. It all depends on how much propagation you plan to undertake. Beware of underestimating your enthusiasm, however, which will only get greater.

Heating an entire greenhouse on frosty nights is expensive, but look at it in the context of the entire twelve months. Guesstimate how many nights are below freezing, then work it out realistically with two max:min thermometers. Put one inside and the other outside. Then calculate exactly how many degrees of frost the basic greenhouse will keep off anyway. Glass should keep off roughly 3–4°C (37–39°F) of frost. Make your decision based on the number of nights when the air in the greenhouse would dip below 0°C (32°F) or, more realistically, below 4°C (39°F).

The heating thermostat should be set to about 4°C (39°F) to allow for the temperature to fall away the further the plants are from the heat source. Fan heaters distribute the warmed air evenly around the greenhouse very effectively and are simple and safe to use. Improved air circulation also helps to prevent airborne fungal disease: a particular problem in a cold, damp winter. In the summer months, the fan can be switched on without the heating element to improve air circulation on hot, humid summer days.

Paraffin and propane heaters are very effective, but can be more cumbersome to use, as well as having the propensity to run out without warning. Electric radiant tubular heaters are cheap but the heat is not circulated, although they can be useful in a much smaller space, such as a partitioned section.

Bench Heating

Heating cuttings from below speeds up the rooting process, enabling the propagator to increase the number of cuttings rooted in a season. It is also very helpful in rooting difficult subjects, increasing the percentage of successful cuttings. If you plan to raise lots of exotic plants from seed, a heated bench will ensure their germination. Bottom heat is also an essential part of the process of bench grafting.

The most up-to-date method is with a thermostatically controlled propagation panel. The heating element is laminated between sheets of heavy foil. This ensures that the heat is spread evenly under the containers without any hot spots or cold corners. The mats are available in standard sizes to fit most benching, or the manufacturers can make them to measure.

Maintenance

The greenhouse will need ventilating every day of the year, summer and winter, unless it is very windy or very cold. In high winds it is essential that the greenhouse is tightly closed up: if the wind gets inside it can cause mayhem and even explode the greenhouse. If the temperature outside during the day is lower than 5°C (41°F), then the thermostat on the heater, set at 4°C (39°F), will switch on and your heating bills for warming up the whole garden will know no bounds.

Ventilation reduces the temperature in summer and winter. If plants are too hot in summer they will not grow. If they are too hot in winter they could be pushed into growth at an inappropriate time, becoming weak and thin.

Ventilation also reduces the levels of humidity in the greenhouse, which is especially important in winter to combat fungal disease. Water also retains its temperature longer than the surrounding air. An unventilated, damp greenhouse in winter therefore will be colder than a dry one and will take more fuel to warm up. In hot weather, as the temperature rises, open the door and windows, then the roof vents first before the side vents; follow this routine the other way round as the temperature falls.

In summer, the glass will need shading to reduce the intensity of the ultraviolet rays. The simplest and cheapest way is to buy a packet of whitening to paint on the top panes and the upper sides. The white deflects the ultraviolet very effectively, with the result that the plants inside are cooled and shaded. A more decorative alternative is to fit purpose-made blinds, although these can be expensive. They will need to be easy to clean thoroughly and should also be detachable for the winter.

The end of summer often marks a transition in the propagation calendar and it is a very good time to give the greenhouse a thorough cleaning inside and out. Remove all the plants first. Who knows what chemical in the disinfectant they might react to? Then use a purpose-made disinfectant to wash out the inside of the panes, the framework and the benching. The outside should also be washed carefully with an extendable window cleaner in order to remove all the green algae that will have accumulated on the glass. (A few drops of bleach in the water helps to keep it off.) The colour green to plants is like black to the human eye: it creates intense shade. Do not use ladders to reach the top of the greenhouse. Falling through ordinary glass from a ladder is potentially fatal and even safety glass breaks and will have to be replaced. When the glass is clean and shiny, replace the plants. They will enjoy a bright and, hopefully, disease-free winter.

The Polytunnel

It is a common misunderstanding that a polytunnel is simply a cheap version of a greenhouse. It is not. It mostly has different uses and is not essential to the amateur propagator. It's all a matter of scale. A cold frame fulfils the same functions, takes up less space and is cheaper and easier to put up. A polytunnel in an attractive garden is an eyesore. All that shiny white polythene gets green and shabby

within a few years and it needs to be screened from the rest of the garden.

The fluctuating temperatures inside a polytunnel cause a lot of condensation, which then drips down the sides of the polythene walls and off the aluminium framework. Therefore any polytunnel needs as much ventilation as possible.

But a polytunnel is much cheaper than a greenhouse and is fairly easy to erect. It takes more brawn than brain. However, the polythene cover only has a life of three to five years before it will need re-cladding. Beyond that, the polythene will downgrade and become clouded.

The uses of a small polytunnel are many and various. It is primarily used to shelter newly potted young plants from too much rain and wind. Once the plants have filled their pots, they can be hardened off outside the tunnel before planting in the garden.

Choosing a Polytunnel
In a garden, the size of the polytunnel will depend on the location to a great extent, but note that low tunnels promote backache, while long ones can suffer from a lack of ventilation in the middle.

A frost-free greenhouse in spring.

Siting

Hitherto, polytunnels did not need planning permission. They were classed as temporary structures and so long as they were at a distance from the road and the neighbours, they were permissible. However, the law in general is changing and the bylaws in particular are different in every Planning Authority. So it is important to check with the local Planning Department first. It is particularly advisable to consult first in a Conservation Area, or if your or your neighbours' houses are listed buildings.

Just like a greenhouse, a polytunnel should be in the sunniest site available and out of the prevailing wind. And, as mentioned above, the polytunnel will not be pretty, so you may prefer to screen it from view of the house and garden.

Materials

The frame of a polytunnel is constructed with tensile steel and should be galvanized inside and out. All the metal fittings should be galvanized, zinc-plated or coated. The diameter of the steel tubing varies a little, but if you intend constructing a tunnel in a windy site or somewhere vulnerable to heavy snow, it would be wise to check the manufacturer's specifications. The basic frame can be strengthened with crop bars and storm stay-braces to prevent the frame from twisting in high winds.

The framework is covered with polythene made with an ultraviolet inhibitor to give it a longer life. There are different grades to choose from, but 720 gauge (180 microns) polythene should last for about four years. A new cover will equate to approximately 15 to 20 per cent of the initial cost of the polytunnel. When the tunnel has to be recovered, the old cover can be effectively recycled by cutting it up into smaller covers for cloches or cold frames.

The polytunnel could be entirely made of polythene to the ground, or it could have a netting partition like a skirt along the bottom. This greatly aids ventilation at the level it is needed: among the plants. At one or both ends there will be a door set into a frame. The timber used for the frames and doors must be tannalized to protect it from rotting, woodworm and so on. Usually, the floor is covered with a woven membrane that prevents weed growth while allowing the passage of water. This is pegged down or held in place by the doors with timber battens.

Construction

To construct a polytunnel is not as difficult as perhaps a greenhouse or a kitchen cupboard. You just need two or three fine days, a set of tools, stepladders and plenty of tall, brawny friends. The instructions are detailed and there is usually a helpline to call if you hit any unforeseen snags or problems.

Irrigation

The easiest way to irrigate the plants is of course by using a hose with a spray head attached. However, a snaking line of hose pulled down the paths between the plants is liable to do some damage unless those paths are wide and therefore consume a lot of space.

It is sensible, if you can afford it, to invest in an overhead irrigation system that can be installed when the tunnel is constructed. This can be attached to a hose from the outside. According to the size of the polytunnel, you will need either one central spray line, or two: one on either side. The water pressure will dictate how many sprays or lines can be operated at one time. Usually, a tap is incorporated into each spray line to shut off the flow in each pipe and keep up the pressure in the pipe that is open.

Lower spray lines that are at knee- or waist-height and drip systems are not usually fitted inside a polytunnel. They are more problematic on a larger scale than on a greenhouse bench, unless you are going to use the polytunnel for growing vegetables.

Sprayers of any sort, however, always describe a circular pattern of irrigation. As you get to know your system you will discover the dry corners. These will of course need to be watered separately on a regular basis, unless you put drought-loving plants in these places, or pots of bulbs in their dormant season.

Maintenance

Ventilation is the major task on a daily basis. The doors should be opened every day, but closed at night to prevent large animals, such as cats and foxes, from getting in. This should be done throughout the year unless there are high winds that could wrench off the doors and damage the door frames. The greatest danger then is that the wind will get inside and contort the steel frame, so shut the tunnel up tight if high winds are forecast. In a gale, commercial growers have been known to slash the polythene sides with a knife to prevent such expensive damage. Tunnels with a netting skirt that reaches 60cm (2ft) up from the ground are perfectly safe in a gale, as the wind simply passes straight through the net and out the other side at a low level.

Watering will be another daily task in the summer; it is best undertaken in the evening. This allows the plants to take up the moisture during the hours of darkness. Then, like the plants inside a greenhouse, as the winter months approach the watering should be reduced, until by mid-winter the polytunnel will only need irrigating about once a week. As ever, plants should be kept on the dry side during the winter to prevent the build-up of fungal disease. Keep an eye on the weather forecast and try to water when there is no risk of frost. It is better that the plants go thirsty than their roots freeze.

During spring and early autumn, you will need to wash the green algae off the tunnel to prevent it shading the plants. There are good products on the market to help delay the build-up of algae, but just a bucket of water with some liquid detergent and an extendable window-cleaning brush should clean the polythene adequately.

Cold Frames

If your aims are more modest than to fill a polytunnel with plants, a cold frame or two will fit the bill well. They are smaller, lower and less obtrusive than an elephantine polytunnel in the garden. They are also adaptable and the sturdier ones will give a greater measure of protection against the frost than a polytunnel. In addition, they are cheap and easy to erect.

Choosing a Cold Frame
A traditional cold frame is pent-shaped, that is, rectangular and taller at the back than the front. The top lifts off or hinges up to provide ventilation. The frame can be constructed of four solid walls of breeze block, treated timber or cedar wood. Alternatively, it can be constructed of rust-proof aluminium, or occasionally tubular steel, and glazed to the ground. Toughened glass, twin-walled polypropylene or polycarbonate are the safest materials to use for glazing, especially if there are children in

the garden. Plain horticultural glass can be very hazardous at knee height and dangerous in such a relatively light structure.

Cedar-wood frames are classy and expensive and look well in any garden context. They come in all sizes to suit any position and manufacturers offer them with toughened glass.

One cold frame is useful. Two or three are much more so: they are adaptable. Each frame could contain young plants that are at the same stage of growth, making it simpler to give each frame the correct ventilation or shading.

Siting
Just like a greenhouse, a cold frame needs to be sited in a sunny spot that is well protected against the wind. They are light structures that will simply take

Pent-shaped cold frames with lids lifted.

Toughened glass aluminium frames.

off in a gale, scattering plants and frames to the four corners of the garden. A row of frames could fit snugly against the low wall of a greenhouse if it is not glazed to the ground. They look quite attractive if they are constructed of the same materials as the greenhouse.

Another good option is to place a tall, upright frame against a sunny south- or west-facing wall of the house. The greater height will allow for shelving that will house more plants per square metre of ground space. The wall of the house will radiate warmth and keep the frame frost-free. On exceptionally frosty nights or in the colder parts of the UK, the plants could be protected with a layer of horticultural fleece until milder weather returns.

Construction

It is advisable to put the cold frame down on a solid level base either of concrete, paving slabs or bare earth. Some frames can be screwed or pinned to the base: an important point in a windy location. On bare earth the ground should be covered with a woven membrane to keep down the weeds and allow for drainage. The ground should be level. If it is bumpy or uneven not only do the plants sit at awkward angles and grow crookedly, but they are also vulnerable to visitations from flat-headed mice, which can squeeze through the thinnest of gaps if given the incentive of a free lunch.

It is not difficult to build a pent-shaped cold frame out of breeze blocks, but the snag is making or finding the Dutch lights for the cover. If you are

a handy carpenter lights can be made and glazed with horticultural-grade glass for very little cost. The whole construction will be solid and cheap. Because the walls are made of breeze blocks it is possible to fill the frame with horticultural grit to the depth of a 1ltr (5in) pot: a plunge bed. This is very useful for vernalizing seed, that is, exposing them to frost. Also, the grit keeps the temperature even around the base of the pots or trays of seed, so that when they have germinated their roots will not experience a fluctuation of temperature from deep frost to gas mark 3.

However, for the less adept at DIY there are plenty of prefabricated cold frames on the market that are very easy to put together. As with greenhouses and polytunnels, their instructions are simple to follow and need very few tools other than a large screwdriver and a spanner. A pair of stout gloves is essential too if the lights are made of toughened glass.

Maintenance

Just as with a greenhouse or polytunnel, ventilation is the most important daily duty. Unless it is windy, lift open the light (the glazed lid) and prop it up. If it is blowing a gale, keep the frame tight shut with a secure catch. It might even be worth making wire ties to anchor the lids down in a windy spot.

The plants will also need watering regularly: every day in summer, winding down to once a week in winter. Keep the plants on the dry side in winter and try to water them when there are no frosts forecast for a few days. Be careful to water the plants at the back of the frame well. Even if the lid is open they are in its rain-shadow.

If severe frosts are forecast overnight, put a loose covering of horticultural fleece over the plants in the afternoon. The air will be trapped under the fleece and kept a few degrees warmer than the ambient temperature. Remove the fleece during the daytime and ventilate the frame if possible. Night frosts often occur when the air is still and the days are bright and sunny, so there is not usually any danger of daytime damage. However, during prolonged periods of snow and sub-zero temperatures in the daytime, keep everything well fleeced and shut tight. And take the necessary precautions against stowaway mice.

In summer, remove the lids completely. If the lids are left on, the little plants will quickly frazzle up in the sun. The glazed lids could be replaced with rigid green netting pinned onto purpose-made frames if shade is required. Soft, loose netting tends to catch at the leaves of the plants inside the frame and pull them out of their compost.

Keep the glass or polypropylene clean to maximize the light. The sides of a frame that is glazed to the ground quickly get muddy. Plants can grow tall and leggy trying to find their way out of the gloom.

A Potting Shed

Perhaps not an absolute essential at the outset, a potting shed, providing it does not become a glory-hole, should be large enough to contain not just a potting bench, but space to store pots, trays and bags of compost. With an electric light and a radio it's a snug, dry place to escape the worst of the weather and get on with the propagation.

Choosing a Potting Shed

Your choice of potting shed will depend on the space you have chosen, how much you want to pay and what's easily available. For the purposes of propagation and potting, a simple basic shed will suffice, preferably with a window for some natural light. You will need to decide whether or not to buy a shed with a wooden floor, or whether to lay a concrete hard-standing as a base. The latter is easier to sweep clean without collecting debris in the cracks, but the former is more comfortable on the feet.

Wooden sheds should be made of treated, tannalized timber and carry a guarantee, but there are plastic and galvanized steel sheds on the market that may be cheaper and simpler to erect. Construction can be carried out by the manufacturer provided that a base is in place before delivery. If the shed is to have a timber floor rather than concrete, the base will need to be well-compacted with hardcore, level and square. DIY construction is often a cheaper option, but sometimes the manufacturers include the cost of construction in the price.

Equipping a Shed

Once your new shed is in place you can fit a potting bench along one side using a sheet of tannalized timber fixed to the wooden walls with upright posts for stability: the bench is going to hold lots of damp, heavy compost and plants. Plastic or steel sheds will need special fixings for shelving, or a free-standing bench. The shelving is useful to house plant pots and trays up and out of the way. A small table or

The potting shed.

shelf to put down secateurs, knives, labels and so on is always useful. An electric power point and an overhead light are useful.

Maintenance

There is usually very little maintenance required with any sort of shed. Cleanliness is next to godliness, however. A messy shed is not only difficult to work in, but harbours all sorts of pests and diseases. Rats and mice have been known to make themselves at home for the winter in rolls of fleece and surplus capillary matting flung down in a corner.

Electric Propagators

There is a range of propagators available at a range of prices. At the cheaper end there are simple deep trays with clear, ventilated domes that fit on top. These are very useful for raising seeds such as hardy annuals and taking cuttings that do not need bottom heat but do need the protection of the dome, such as tender perennial cuttings. These propagators could fit on a windowsill or within a greenhouse.

There are also propagators which maintain a thermostatically controlled bottom heat at an already fixed temperature that is about right for the majority of seeds, although sometimes the heat can be a little high for cuttings. Also, the thermostats are not very precise: the temperature can fluctuate rather widely. The domes are ventilated.

At the top of the price range there are the thermostatically controlled propagators with a wider, more

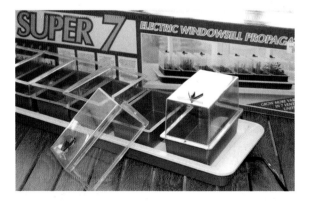

Electric propagating trays for a windowsill.

accurate temperature range, controlled by a sensor that is inserted into the potting compost linked to a thermostat. Many use a foil mat that will heat up evenly and should be covered with a layer of capillary matting for protection. Others have a mat that has heating cables inserted like an electric blanket. If you buy one of these, it would be wise to cover the mat with thick foil or a layer of sand to distribute the heat more evenly, or there will be marked hot spots. These larger propagators often have a clear, ultraviolet-stabilized plastic cover that zips open to access the plants and provide ventilation. These propagators can be used for a wide range of cuttings and raising seed. An added advantage is that the whole contraption will fold up and can be put away tidily when it's not in use.

Maximum:Minimum Thermometers

A max:min thermometer will register the coldest and the hottest temperature recorded since it was previously set, enabling you to check the exact temperatures within the greenhouse or polytunnel overnight or during a very hot day. Over time, you will learn the difference between what temperatures, be they high or low, are predicted by the weather forecasters and what to expect inside the greenhouse.

Use such a thermometer to keep an eye on high temperatures in the summer. Excessive heat can then be alleviated by dousing greenhouse paths with cool water and spraying young plants overhead.

If you want to work out precisely how many degrees of frost your greenhouse protects against, use two thermometers. Set one within the structure and the other outside in the shade. Fix them to wood rather than a metal frame, if possible. Check the difference every morning for a week, comparing the different temperatures inside and outside. The greenhouse will probably give up to 4° or 5°C (39° or 41°F) protection; the polytunnel will be about the same temperature as outside.

Protective Materials

Horticultural Fleece

As has been mentioned above, horticultural fleece is worth more than its light weight in gold. Placed loosely over vulnerable plants, it will give several degrees of frost protection. This is especially true in late spring when young growth is already visible, but very soft and vulnerable even on the hardiest plants.

Shading

The colour green is dark shade to a plant. If the sun is scorching young leaves, throw a piece of netting over the top to spare their blushes and burns. Remove it carefully, however, so that those leaves are not snagged by the netting.

Rigid green netting can be pinned to a wooden frame to place on top of a cold frame, or it can be attached to a larger walk-in frame to provide protection for young shade- loving plants. Heavy-duty netting can even be used to cover a polytunnel frame, although the netting downgrades with algae and would have to be replaced every three or four years.

Windbreak Material

This is made of strips of heavy-duty green or black polythene and is available in different grades according to how much reduction of wind speed is required. It is unsightly, but useful while a hedge is being grown to replace it eventually.

Pots and Containers

The advent of plastic pots brought about a sea-change in commercial horticulture in the 1970s. Up until that time, everyone used, and reused, terracotta pots. The porous nature of terracotta absorbs fungal spores, weed seeds and pest eggs that regenerate however well the pots are cleaned. (Cleaning pots beats washing-up as the least amusing chore.) They are also expensive, breakable and very heavy.

Plastic pots have been revolutionary. They are cheap enough to buy new every time you propagate and pot up. If you want to recycle them, cleaning is easier and more effective. And providing you don't jump on them, plastic pots are tough. They are also light enough to carry several at once in a tray, which saves time and your back.

Some would say that porous terracotta is better for rooting cuttings. It is a rather subjective judgment and there are other more important factors

Plastic pots.

that markedly do influence rooting. But even simple, basic terracotta pots are lovely for potting up a few spring bulbs to put on the windowsill, and have a functional beauty when filled with summer perennials.

On balance, plastic pots win hands down for propagation, but there are one or two other alternatives. Compressed peat pots are a bit like puff pastry. They are small and flat, with an inner circle stamped on the middle, and are contained within a fine gauze mesh. When they are dropped into a bucket of water they swell and become vol-au-vents: just right for inserting cuttings. However, the drainage is questionable; they dry out alarmingly fast; and are probably most useful for rooting very easy subjects such as fuchsias. And many gardeners have a dislike of using peat.

Terracotta pots.

Seed trays.

Pot-shaped pots can also be made of peat. There are also rice-paper pots made from the rice-paper tree: *Tetrapanax papyrifer*, or pots manufactured from other bio-degradable materials. (Jiffy pots make a range of peat and peat-free pots.) When the plant is ready, the whole pot can be planted or potted on. The roots will grow through it, although it is wise to make sure that the lip of the pot is broken off so that it does not act as a wick and dry out the root system. Mostly, these pots have their limitations of size, cost and availability. Eventually, biodegradable plastic might hit the garden market, but so far it has proved too costly.

So reusing cleaned plastic pots is a tempting idea, but beware of collecting, or buying, too many different-sized pots of whatever material. When you stand them down to grow on, it is much easier if all the pots in a given area are the same size. Round pots will interlock to use the available space, although square-cut pots are more space-efficient. Where there are spaces at ground level between the pots, there will be greedy little mice setting up home. So beg, borrow or buy as few different sizes and shapes as possible.

Seed trays come in different sizes. The standard rectangular shape will hold four times five cuttings of pricked-out seedlings perfectly, unless they are especially big cuttings like hydrangeas, or have large roots like hellebores. For fewer seedlings, or smaller cuttings like thyme or heather, a half tray will hold the same number: twenty. There is even a quarter-sized tray, but that does have its limitations. Clearly,

the larger the tray, the greater the number of seeds it will contain without sowing them too densely. There are also larger, deeper trays available with irrigation holes that are perfect for holding tubers, such as dahlias, during the winter.

However, for large cuttings, such as hydrangeas, it is probably wiser to use individual small square pots that will keep each cutting apart from its neighbours while they are rooting, rather than a large tray. While these small pots will take up more space on the bench or propagating tray, any failures can be extracted without disturbing the remainder of the batch.

Cell trays, or plugs, are extremely useful for sowing seeds of plants that dislike root disturbance, such as annual poppies. A pinch of seed in each cell germinates and is thinned to just one or two seedlings per plug, which can be further reduced to one. Then the whole plug – roots, shoots and all – is ready for planting without interfering with the fine roots.

Cell trays are also excellent for root cuttings of oriental poppies and Japanese anemones, which easily part company with their shoots when they are handled. The trays are available in various sizes and numbers of plugs, and are made of polystyrene or heavy-duty plastic. They can be very tricky to clean thoroughly, however, and it is wiser to buy cheap trays that can be discarded, rather than risk the transmission of pest and disease from one crop to the next. Jiffy also makes peat and peat-free cellular strips that biodegrade thousands of years faster than discarded plastic.

Plug trays.

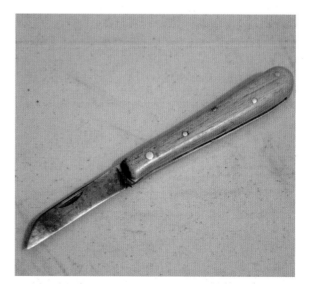

Secateurs and knives.

Small Tools

Assuming that the usual gardener's arsenal of spades and forks is already to hand, it is merely a matter of adding to the collection an old pair and a good pair of secateurs, a large old knife, an old penknife and a very sharp knife for taking cuttings. Perhaps an ancient dinner fork for lifting seedlings would also prove useful.

As with all things, the more that a pair of secateurs costs, the better it will be. A good pair of secateurs for propagation and pruning should have a scissor-cut action. Blade and anvil secateurs are only useful for cutting flowers for the house. A scissor action will give a clean cut, provided the blades are kept sharp, whereas an anvil cut will crush the stems of the plant and the cutting. Choose a pair of secateurs with carbon steel blades rather than stainless steel, so that they can be sharpened with a whet-stone. The blade should be angled or bevelled on one side and flat on the other for ease of sharpening. Felco makes the gold-standard secateurs that can be taken apart for cleaning, sharpening and oiling with a special spanner. They will also service them for a very small fee, including postage. Such secateurs are worth the investment.

A hand axe, an old bread knife and a sturdy blunt penknife are very useful for dividing everything from *Miscanthus* to tubers and tight herbaceous crowns like hostas; in fact, anything that is covered in soil. Nothing blunts a sharp blade more quickly than grains of soil.

The most important item is a cuttings knife: one that can be kept razor sharp. It should therefore be made of carbon steel. The blade should be straight for taking cuttings, or narrow, pointed and slightly curved for grafting. Tina knives are renowned for their workmanship and their ability to hold an edge. Each knife is hand-forged and the shaped walnut handle sits in the hand comfortably. Brass liners and pins give the handle the strength needed to take all types of cuttings or grafts. They are much more expensive than the competition, but they last in perfect condition for a lifetime.

A well-used Tina knife.

Propagation Calendar

The propagation year in the UK falls naturally into a pattern according to the seasons. But these days, the seasons seem to be changing. The seasons also vary considerably from north to south of the UK and to a lesser extent from east to west. Altitude is also a factor: as a rough guide, spring arrives two days later, and autumn two days earlier, for every 30m (100ft) rise in height above sea level. This Appendix uses the gardens of the Royal Horticultural Society at Wisley in Surrey as a benchmark.

It is wiser to gauge the advancement of each season by the way plants behave in reaction to the prevailing weather patterns, than to be too pedantic about the months. Spring is heralded by a faint flush of green in the hedgerows and the germination of wild flower seedlings or weeds as the soil warms to above 10°C (50°F). Autumn is accompanied by the first frosts at night and the colouring of deciduous foliage as the days become shorter than the nights.

The months given below are therefore merely a guide and local conditions should always be taken into account.

MARCH

Frost at night, but by day the soil temperature is beginning to warm.

Propagation

- Finish dividing herbaceous perennials and alpine plants by the end of March.
- Finish bench-grafting acers, rhododendrons and so on.
- Finish making approach grafts on espalier fruit trees.
- Finish lifting and dividing hardy ferns.
- Sow hardy annuals outside where they are to flower.
- Sow half-hardy annuals under glass (that is, frost-free).
- Sow primula seed that has been stored overwinter in the fridge.
- Sow seed of Mediterranean plants such as herbs.
- Lift and divide snowdrops while their foliage is visible.
- Make layers of suitable plants.
- Detach rooted shoots of heathers that have been mounded with peat during the winter months and pot them up.
- Divide and repot canna lilies in a frost-free greenhouse.
- Divide and replant or pot up ornamental grasses.
- Divide and cut up bergenia rhizomes.

Other Tasks

- Continue potting on overwintered plants and those needing to grow on another year.
- Pot up seedlings of pelargoniums sown in December and January.
- Pot up heather cuttings.
- Pot up root cuttings when they have made sufficient root growth.
- Pot up alpines and any softwood cuttings that were too late last September and give them a haircut with a pair of secateurs.
- Plant out in a nursery those hardwood cuttings that were rooted in deep pots.
- Pot up lily seedlings as they appear.
- Start dahlias into growth in the frost-free greenhouse.

Dogwood and snowdrops (March).

APRIL

Frosts at night remain a threat, but the soil temperature is warm and the days are longer than the nights: spring.

Propagation

- Take basal cuttings of asters, delphiniums, *Campanula lactiflora* and so on when the bottom growth reaches about 15cm (6in).
- Take dahlia cuttings.
- Sow seed of alpines, herbaceous perennials and ornamental grasses.
- Sow seed of exotics that need warmth to germinate and place in a heated propagator.
- Continue to make layers of suitable plants.
- Divide snowdrops before their foliage dies down for the summer.

Other Tasks

- Prick out and pot up seedlings sown last month.
- Continue to pot up heather cuttings.
- Continue to pot up root cuttings.
- Examine semi-ripe evergreen cuttings taken last autumn and either liquid-feed them, or, if they have rooted well, pot them up.
- Inspect the layers made last spring. Lift and pot them up if they have made sufficient root.

MAY

There is still a risk of night-time frost. Perennials, trees and shrubs are in active growth. Spring-flowering bulbs are setting seed and beginning to die down.

- Sow seed of hardy biennials for flowering next year.

Tulips and spring flowers (April).

- Sow short-viability seed, such as pulsatillas and cyclamen, when they ripen.
- Take cuttings of clematis as soon as the growth has firmed up enough.
- Continue to layer suitable plants.

Other Tasks

- Prick out and pot up seedlings sown last month.
- Pot up basal cuttings, including dahlias, taken last month.
- Pot up seedlings of alpines and herbaceous perennials sown last month.
- Pot on and stake young clematis that were propagated last year.
- Pot up semi-ripe cuttings of evergreens taken last autumn.
- Pot up bergenia rhizomes.
- Continue to inspect the layers made last spring. Lift and pot them up when they have made sufficient root.

- Harden off and plant out hardy annuals that have been raised indoors.

JUNE

All risk of frost is past. Spring-flowering bulbs have become dormant. The leaves in the hedgerow have matured and darkened. The tree canopy covers the woodland floor. Midsummer Day marks the change in day length.

Propagation

- Take softwood cuttings of alpines.
- Take softwood cuttings of lilacs, prunus, *Rubus spectabilis*, philadelphus, weigela and hydrangeas when the weather is cool and damp.
- Take cuttings of Mediterranean evergreens such as cistus and silver-leaved evergreens such as lavender, sage and rosemary.

Allium christophii *in flower (May)*.

Rosa *'Rambling Rector' (June)*.

- Continue to take clematis cuttings.
- Divide bearded irises after flowering.
- Take leaf cuttings of begonias and African violets.
- Collect and sow seed of oriental hellebores immediately they are ripe.
- Collect and sow spores of ferns as they become available.
- Finish making layers of suitable plants.
- Dig up named snowdrops in pots and propagate them by cutting up the bulbs.

Other Tasks

- Plant out dahlia cuttings.
- Finish planting out half-hardy annuals.
- Plant out biennials in a nursery bed.

JULY

One of the hottest months of the year, potentially. Ventilation and watering will be the major daily tasks.

Propagation

- Sow primula seed as soon as it is ripe.
- Continue to take softwood cuttings in damp, cool weather.
- Divide bearded iris rhizomes.
- Divide epimediums.
- Start budding family fruit trees and top-worked shrubs and roses.
- Collect and sow fern spores as they become available.

Summer perennial border (July).

Other Tasks

- Collect seed from early flowering perennials and grasses.
- Collect primula seed as it ripens and either store it or sow it immediately.

AUGUST

Another of the hottest months: ventilation and watering are again the major daily tasks.

Propagation

- In a cool spell take softwood cuttings of tender perennials such as pelargoniums, fuchsias and osteospermums.

- Take softwood cuttings of heathers.
- Pot up softwood cuttings taken earlier in the year.
- Divide Siberian irises and *Iris ensata* after flowering.
- Finish budding family fruit trees and top-worked shrubs and roses.

Other Tasks

- Pot on oriental hellebores.

SEPTEMBER

The season can vary considerably this month. In most years it is a late summer month, but in others it can be the start of autumn. Be prepared for night-time frosts. The nights are longer than the days from mid-month.

Hydrangea macrophylla *(August)*.

Propagation

- Finish taking softwood cuttings of tender perennials.
- Take semi-ripe cuttings of evergreens such as bay *(Laurus nobilis)*, box *(Buxus sempervirens)*, holly *(Ilex aquifolium)* and *Viburnum tinus*.
- Lift and divide herbaceous perennials on light soils if the weather is cool and damp.
- Sow seed of perennials that need a cold period to germinate (stratification).
- Sow hypogeal lily seed in a frost-free greenhouse.

Late summer perennial border (September).

Other Tasks

- Pot up softwood cuttings of tender perennials taken last month. Leave any that are not sufficiently rooted in their propagation trays until next spring.
- Pot up leaf cuttings before the end of the month and keep them frost-free.
- Finish potting up softwood cuttings taken earlier in the year before the end of the month.
- Collect seed from perennials, grasses and dahlias as they ripen.
- Plant out hardy biennials where they are to flower.
- Plant out perennials and shrubs if they are large enough.

OCTOBER

The first true month of autumn. The day length is shortening. There are night-time frosts.

Propagation

- Lift and divide hardy herbaceous on light soils.
- Take semi-ripe cuttings of evergreens.

Other Tasks

- Collect seed of perennials and grasses on a dry day.
- Lift and store dahlia tubers when their foliage is brought down by frost.
- Finish planting out hardy biennials.
- Plant out in their final positions those hardwood cuttings that were taken last winter and rooted and grown on outside.
- Cover mature clumps of heather with mounds of peat/peat substitute to induce them to root.
- Take trays of lily seed sown six weeks earlier outside for a six-week cold period.

NOVEMBER

Autumn ends. Leaves drop off deciduous trees and herbaceous foliage dies back completely. The days are short.

Ornamental grasses in autumn (October).

Dewy mornings (November).

The light levels are low. Frosts can occur at night and last throughout the day. Plants stop growing when the daily mean temperature falls below 6°C (43°F).

Propagation

- Finish taking semi-ripe cuttings of evergreens.
- Take hardwood cuttings of dogwoods, willows, flowering currants and soft fruit bushes.
- Root fernlets that arise on varieties of *Polystichum setiferum*.

Other Tasks

- Cut back the top growth on potted clematis cuttings to two pairs of buds.

DECEMBER

Midwinter and the shortest day. Light levels are at their lowest. Plants are mostly dormant. Gales and rain are common. Frosts occur day or night. However, December

Low winter sun sidelights the border (December).

is rarely the coldest month. A period of cold early in the month often presages a mild winter. Cold weather at the end of the month can be the start of a hard winter.

Propagation

- Sow seed of alpines and other perennials that need a period of cold before germination.
- Start sowing seed of pelargoniums at the end of the month in a heated propagator.
- Lift suitable perennials and take root cuttings.
- Take hardwood cuttings of suitable shrubs.
- Root fernlets on varieties of *Polystichum setiferum*.

Other Tasks

- Ventilate the greenhouse and garden frames, especially on sunny days.
- Water in the mornings when the weather is generally frost-free.
- Keep plants on the dry side: don't overwater.
- Bring trays of lily seed that have been stratifying into a frost-free greenhouse.

JANUARY

The coldest part of the winter is often the end of this month and the beginning of February. Light levels are very low. Frosts occur day or night.

Propagation

- Continue sowing seed of alpines and perennials that require a period of frost.
- Sow seed of pelargoniums in a heated propagator.
- Continue to take root cuttings of suitable plants.
- Take semi-ripe cuttings of conifers such as juniper that root easily.

Other Tasks

- Ventilate the greenhouse and garden frames, especially on sunny days.
- Water in the mornings when the weather is generally frost-free.
- Keep plants on the dry side: don't overwater.

Winter (January).

FEBRUARY

On warm days, spring is in the air, but if the weather systems are coming from the east, winter is not yet over. Westerly airstreams bring rain and gales, but not snow and ice. The days are lengthening and the sun is getting higher in the sky at midday.

Propagation

- Lift and divide herbaceous perennials especially on heavy soil.
- Lift and divide hardy ferns.
- Bench-graft acers, rhododendrons and so on.

Hellebores (February).

- Make approach grafts on espalier fruit trees.
- Sow seed of hardy annuals in the green-house.
- In the greenhouse, sow seed of half-hardy annuals such as *Nicotiana* that take a long time to germinate.
- Continue to take semi-ripe cuttings of conifers.
- Continue to take root cuttings.

Other Tasks

- Start potting on overwintered plants and those needing to grow on another year.

Hardiness Zones

The Hardiness Zones shown here have been devised by the United States Department of Agriculture. The chart shows the average annual minimum temperature of each zone.

Most of the British Isles lies within Zone 8. Cornwall, western and southern coastal areas and central London lie within Zone 9, while the Highlands of Scotland are Zone 7. However, zones are rated only by temperature. Some plants will survive colder temperatures than those indicated if they experience drier conditions.

HARDINESS ZONES

Zone	Celsius	Fahrenheit
1	below −45	below −50
2	−45 to −40	−50 to −40
3	−40 to −34	−40 to −30
4	−34 to −29	−30 to −20
5	−29 to −23	−20 to −10
6	−23 to −18	−10 to 0
7	−18 to −12	0 to 10
8	−12 to −7	10 to 20
9	−7 to −1	20 to 30
10	−1 to 4	30 to 40
11	above 4	above 40

Glossary

Abscissic acid
Deciduous plants shed their leaves in autumn in response to the build-up during the summer of abscissic acid in the plant. This forms a layer of cork cells across the base of the leaf stem where it joins the main stem, called the abscission layer. As the layer thickens, the leaf becomes detached and falls off.

Air porosity
Soils and composts need air within their structures to provide oxygen to the roots so that they can respire. Compost with low air porosity will be heavy and wet, with few small spaces between the soil particles. The roots will only grow very slowly. Compost with high air porosity will be light, fluffy and well drained, leaving large spaces between the soil particles. The spaces could become filled with soil pests or fungal spores that could damage the roots.

Annual
A plant that grows from seed, flowers and sets its own seed within the space of one year. It can only be propagated by seed, not by taking cuttings.

Anthocyanin
The red pigment in leaves and plants, such as coloured-leaf pelargoniums.

Aphicide
A compound, chemical or non-chemical, that is formulated to target blackfly, greenfly and other aphids. It will not affect other insects.

Apical dominance
The growing tip of a plant is full of hormones that make the shoot grow upwards rather than branch out sideways at the leaf axils. This apical dominance is very obvious in Christmas trees, making a suitable perch for the Christmas angel.

Auxins
Plant hormones that control growth, abscission, tropisms and other functions. They are produced by the plant in response to light, day length, gravity and temperature, among other factors. They also interact with each other.

Axils – adapted axils
The junction between the leaf stalk and the main stem, often where an axial bud is forming. Rhizomes, which are modified stems, have adapted axils that resemble creases, where the axial buds form.

Basal heat
Heat that comes from beneath via a heated mat or cables. Many cuttings will root faster with heat at the base and a cooler temperature and moisture on their top shoots. Basal heat also mimics tropical soils where endemic seeds germinate.

Basal plate
On a green shoot the basal plate is the swollen stem where a shoot joins the main stem. It is full of phytohormones and is incorporated into a nodal cutting taken with a heel to encourage rooting. Or, it is the bottom of a bulb. This is a modified stem to which the scales of the bulb are attached. These scales are modified leaves.

Biennial
A plant that grows from seed in its first year to form a rosette or crown. In the second year, the flower is produced and seed is set. The plant then dies.

Biological control
The use of benign insects, nematodes, or fungus to predate and destroy specific pests and diseases.

Bulbils
Tiny bulbs that are formed at the base of a bulb attached to the basal plate, or that occur in the leaf axils on the stems.

Calcicole
A plant that grows well in alkaline soils with a high pH and less well in acid soils.

Calcifuge
A plant that grows well in acid soils with a low pH and poorly in alkaline soils.

Cambium
The thin layer just beneath the skin or bark of stems in dicotyledonous plants. The cells in the cambium layer are capable of growing into each other where they make contact in a graft union. Roots emerge from the cambium layer when it is exposed on a cutting.

Chelated iron
Iron particles that have been chemically treated to allow them to be taken up by an acid-loving plant growing in an alkaline soil.

Chlorophyll
The green pigment in leaves and stems that is essential for the process of photosynthesis.

Chlorosis
The yellowing of green leaves between the veins, often symptomatic of a lack of iron on alkaline soils.

Clone
In botanical terms, a plant that is genetically identical to the plant from which it has been generated.

Corms
An adapted stem with thin leaves and axial buds that has swollen to become an underground storage organ.

Cotyledons
The seed leaves that are produced first when a seed germinates. The next leaves will be typical of the mother plant.

Cultivar
A plant that has been produced and named by breeding and selection. Its unique set of genes can only be propagated clonally. The cultivar name is written between inverted commas and comes after the genus and species names (*Papaver orientale* 'Patty's Plum', for example).

Damping off
A virulent fungal disease, usually of seedlings, where a patch of mould appears and spreads quickly to infect the entire batch.

Dicotyledon
A plant that produces two cotyledons (seed leaves).

Dormant
A plant or seed that is alive or viable but not actively growing.

Drench
A pesticide or fungicide that is applied to the soil with a watering can.

Epigeal germination
Seed germination of the shoots that occurs at the same time as the roots (compare this with hypogeal germination).

Ericaceous
Taken to mean lime-hating or calcifuge, its true meaning is pertaining to erica or heather.

Etiolate
To grow tall, pale and weakly in poor light conditions.

Explant
During the process of micropropation the growing tip is cut from a typical plant, removing all contaminants and diseases. The initial plant thus produced is called the explant and this is the mother plant of all the subsequent micropropagated plants produced.

Fastigiate
Growing upright with all the branches parallel to the main trunk or stem.

Genus, genera
A class of plants that is within a family and consists of different species. The genus takes a capital letter *(Papaver orientale* 'Patty's Plum', for example).

Germination
The process by which a seed starts to grow after a period of dormancy.

Gibberellins
A group of around thirty closely related plant hormones that regulate the growth of a plant.

Habit
The manner in which a plant typically grows.

Hardening off
Acclimatizing a plant that has been grown under protection to the higher levels of light and the cooler, fluctuating temperatures outside.

Hardiness
A plant's ability to withstand winter temperatures outside in the UK.

Heel
The tongue of rind or skin on a cutting that has been taken from the base of a side shoot where it joins the main stem.

Herbaceous
Plants that die down completely to the ground during winter. (Plants that leave a woody framework in winter should correctly be called perennial rather than herbaceous.)

Hormone rooting powder or gel
A powder or gel that contains IAA (indoleacetic acid), a growth hormone that promotes the formation of roots in the cambium layer of a cutting. Hormone rooting powder or gel usually also contains a fungicide.

Horticultural grit
Washed river grit that contains no salts to interfere with the process of osmosis in a plant.

Hypogeal germination
The seed germination of the root only in the first spring after sowing. The shoot usually appears in the second spring. (Compare with epigeal germination.)

IAA
Indoleacetic acid is the growth hormone that specifically controls root formation. It is present in hormone rooting powder and gel.

Internodes
The space on a stem between the nodes.

Juvenile
The first stage of growth of a plant before it reaches maturity and is able to flower and set seed. Sometimes plants such as ivy display different foliage when they are juvenile, which changes when the plant becomes mature.

Mature
The second stage of growth of a plant when it is able to flower and set seed.

Meristem
The growing tip of a plant where the cells are dividing actively.

Monocarpic
A plant that flowers only once and then dies. It can take several years to reach the flowering stage. (A biennial, by definition, takes only two seasons to flower.)

Monocotyledon
A plant that produces only one cotyledon (seed leaf).

Node, nodal
The point on a stem where a leaf and axial bud are attached.

Osmosis
The passage of dilute water across a semi-permeable membrane in the plant, usually the root, that is impermeable to the more concentrated solution within the plant. So the passage of water is one way: from the dilute soil water into the concentrated water in the roots.

Perennial
A plant that endures through the winter and does not die when it sets seed.

Perlite
A form of obsidian that is an industrial by-product used in propagation as an inert, water-holding substrate of compost.

Petiole
The stalk that attaches a leaf to the stem.

pH
The name of a logarithmic scale measuring the acidity and alkalinity of a substance.

Phloem
The vascular tissue that moves sugars and other dissolved chemicals down from the leaves.

Photosynthesis
The process by which a plant converts carbon dioxide and water in the presence of sunlight into sugars and other nutrients in the chlorophyll present in its leaves. The by-product of this process is oxygen.

Phytohormones
Plant hormones.

Plug trays
Cellular trays with uniform holes for growing cuttings or seeds with the minimum of root disturbance.

Polarity
The ability of parts of a plant to grow up or down in response to gravity.

Pollination
The point at which the pollen is deposited on the female part of a flower to allow fertilization of the embryo and production of seed.

Potting up/on
The process of putting a rooted cutting or seedling into a pot, or from a smaller pot into a larger one.

Pricking out
The process of separating germinated seedlings and replanting them into a grid pattern in another container of fresh compost.

Reversion
The production of an entirely green shoot on a variegated plant, or returning to the typical form of growth of a plant grown for its atypical habit.

Rhizomes
A thick, fleshy underground stem that has become a storage organ.

Roguing
Removing any visibly atypical seedlings from a tray when their true leaves emerge (for example, pulling out any green-leaved seedlings from a tray of variegated ones).

Rootstock
The part of a grafted plant that bears the roots.

Scion
The part of a grafted plant that bears the desired top growth.

Selfing
The process of self-pollination, that is, the pollen from a flower is placed on the female parts of the same flower.

Sequestered iron
Chelated iron particles that have been chemically treated to allow them to be taken up by an acid-loving plant growing in an alkaline soil.

Slow-release fertilizer
Fertilizer that is contained within semi-porous granules that open in the presence of warmth and moisture over the course of a specified time.

Species
A group of plants within a genus that is capable of interbreeding. A species is written in the lower case after the genus and before the cultivar names (*Papaver orientale* 'Patty's Plum', for example).

Stratification
The process of treating dormant seeds with a period of cold temperatures in order to effect germination.

Tropism
The plant's response to stimuli such as light or gravity.

Tuber
Swollen roots that have formed storage organs, such as potatoes.

Turgid
A plant or leaf that is full of moisture.

Union
The point where the scion is joined to the rootstock in a grafted plant.

Vermiculite
A dark yellow mineral that is an industrial by-product used as a water-retentive substrate of compost.

Viability
The ability to regenerate.

Xylem
Vascular tissue that conducts water and minerals from the roots up the plant to the leaves.

Suggested Additional Reading

Coombes, Allen J., *Dictionary of Plant Names* (Collingridge Books)
Foster, F. Gordon, *Ferns to Know and Grow* (Timber Press)
Gorer, Richard, *Growing Plants from Seed* (Faber Paperbacks)
Grounds, Roger, *Ornamental Grasses* (Christopher Helm)
Dr D. G., Hessayon, *The Pest & Weed Expert* (Transworld Publishers)
Phillips, Roger, and Rix, Martyn, *Perennials, Vols 1 & 2* (Pan Books)
RHS *PlantFinder* (Dorling Kindersley)
Rice, Graham, and Strangman, Elizabeth, *The Gardener's Guide to Growing Hellebores* (David & Charles)
Skellern, Claire, and Rogers, Paul, *Basic Botany* (Macdonald & Evans)

Index

Entries in **bold** refer to illustrations.